Mary W. Hinman Abel

Practical Sanitary and Economic Cooking

Adapted to Persons of Moderate and Small Means

Mary W. Hinman Abel

Practical Sanitary and Economic Cooking
Adapted to Persons of Moderate and Small Means

ISBN/EAN: 9783744792318

Printed in Europe, USA, Canada, Australia, Japan

Cover: Foto ©Andreas Hilbeck / pixelio.de

More available books at **www.hansebooks.com**

PRACTICAL
SANITARY AND ECONOMIC COOKING

ADAPTED TO

PERSONS OF MODERATE AND SMALL MEANS

BY

MRS. MARY HINMAN ABEL.

THE LOMB PRIZE ESSAY.

Inscription: "The Five Food Principles, Illustrated by Practical Recipes."

PUBLISHED BY THE
AMERICAN PUBLIC HEALTH ASSOCIATION.
1890.

PREFACE.

Perhaps there is no better way of presenting to the public the facts which led to the creation of this valuable work, than by inserting the announcement which resulted in the exceedingly lively and able competition for the prize, as well as the merited honor which was certain to fall upon the successful competitor. It read as follows:

AMERICAN PUBLIC HEALTH ASSOCIATION.

THE LOMB PRIZE ESSAYS.

Two Prizes for 1888.

Mr. Henry Lomb, of Rochester, N.Y., now well known to the American public as the originator of the "Lomb Prize Essays," offers, through the American Public Health Association, two prizes for the current year, on the following subject:

PRACTICAL SANITARY AND ECONOMIC COOKING ADAPTED TO PERSONS OF MODERATE AND SMALL MEANS.

First Prize, $500, - - - Second Prize, $200.

JUDGES: Prof. Charles A. Lindsley, New Haven, Conn.; Prof. George H. Rohé, Baltimore, Md.; Prof. Victor C. Vaughan, Ann Arbor, Mich.; Mrs. Ellen H. Richards, Boston, Mass.; Miss Emma C. G. Polson, New Haven, Conn.

CONDITIONS: The arrangement of the essay will be left to the discretion of the author. They are, however, expected to cover, in the broadest and most specific manner, methods of cooking as well as carefully prepared receipts, for three classes,—(1) those of moderate means; (2) those of small means; (3) those who may be called poor. For each of these classes, receipts for three meals a day for several days in succession should be given, each meal to meet the requirements of the body, and to vary as much as possible from day to day. Formulas for at least twelve dinners, to be carried to the place of work, and mostly eaten cold, to be given. Healthfulness, practical arrangement, low cost, and palatableness should be combined considerations. The object of this work is for the information of the housewife, to whose requirements the average cook-book is ill adapted, as well as to bring to her attention healthful and economic methods and receipts.

All essays written for the above prizes must be in the hands of the Secretary, Dr. Irving A. Watson, Concord, N. H., on or before September 15, 1888. Each essay must bear a motto, and have accompanying it a securely sealed envelope containing the author's name and address, with the same motto upon the outside of the envelope.

After the prize essays have been determined upon, the envelopes bearing the mottoes corresponding to the prize essays will be opened, and the awards made to the persons whose names are found within them. The remaining envelopes, unless the corresponding essays are reclaimed by authors or their representatives within thirty days after publication of the awards, will be destroyed, unopened, by the Secretary.

None of the judges will be allowed to compete for a prize.

The judges will announce the awards at the Annual Meeting of the American Public Health Association, 1888.

It is intended that the above essays shall be essentially American in their character and application, and this will be considered by the judges as an especial merit.

Competition is open to authors of any nationality, but all the papers must be in the English language.

IRVING A. WATSON,
Secretary.

CONCORD, N. H., February, 1888.

The above circular was extensively circulated and published throughout the United States and the Dominion of Canada, with the result of bringing to the Secretary, within the specified time, *seventy essays* upon the subject announced. The arrival of these essays covered a period of nearly five months, and they were forwarded to the Chairman of the Committee of Award nearly as fast as received, thus giving the committee ample time for their exceedingly laborious work of examination. The decision of the judges was announced at the Sixteenth Annual Meeting of the American Public Health Association, and was as follows:

REPORT OF COMMITTEE ON THE LOMB PRIZES.

Your committee, to whom were referred the essays upon "Practical Sanitary and Economic Cooking Adapted for Persons of Moderate and Small Means," respectfully report that they have perused with thoughtful and considerate attention the three score and ten essays which were submitted to them.

A few of them were presented in beautiful specimens of type-writing, but the great majority of them were in manuscript, and some of them not in the most legible characters, a circumstance which, it will be appreciated, became an important matter, when considered in connection with the large number of competitors, and the fact that many of their papers were each of several hundred pages in length.

The result of the labors of the committee is, that by unanimous approval, the first prize of $500 is awarded to the author of the essay bearing this inscription,—"The Five Food Principles, illustrated by Practical Recipes."

Your committee would further report that although there were among the remaining sixty-nine a number of essays of considerable merit, there was no single one so prominently superior to others as to commend the approval of the majority of your committee, nor was there any which did not contain some errors of statement, which your committee did not feel justified in endorsing with the approval of this Association by the bestowal of a prize, or else which did not fail to meet some of the conditions upon which the prize was offered, or which was not otherwise objectionable because of literary defects.

Your committee would therefore respectfully report that no essay was found among those submitted to them which they judged deserving of the second prize of $200.

The committee consider it a duty, in awarding the prize, to emphasize the fact that of all the essays submitted the one selected is not only preëminently the best, but that it is also intrinsically an admirable treatise on the subject.

It is simple and lucid in statement, methodical in arrangement, and well adapted to the practical wants of the classes to which it is addressed. Whoever may read it can have confidence in the soundness of its teachings, and cannot fail to be instructed in the art of cooking by its plain precepts, founded as they are upon the correct application of the scientific principles of chemistry and physiology to the proper preparation of food for man.

All of which is respectfully submitted.

C. A. Lindsley.
George H. Rohé.
V. C. Vaughan.
Ellen H. Richards.
Emma C. G. Polson.

The American public is to be congratulated upon this useful and valuable contribution to the needs of its great army of working people, made possible through the humanitarian benevolence of a private citizen. This was the fifth prize offered by the same citizen, through the same channel, for the noble purpose of ameliorating, in some degree, the hardships which befall mankind in the tireless struggle for existence.

That this essay may be placed in the hands of every family in the country, is his earnest desire as well as that of the Association; therefore a price barely covering the cost has been placed upon this volume. It is to be hoped, that Government departments, state and local boards of health, sanitary and benevolent associations, manufacturers, employers, etc., will purchase editions at cost, or otherwise aid in distributing this work among the people.

Although a copyright has been placed upon these essays for legitimate protection, permission to publish under certain conditions, can be obtained by addressing the secretary.

We commend this volume to the public, believing it to be an unequaled work upon "Practical Sanitary and Economic Cooking, adapted to persons of moderate and small means."

Irving A. Watson

Secretary American Public Health Association.

TABLE OF CONTENTS.

INTRODUCTION.

Few things are of more importance than that we should find ourselves physically and mentally equal to our day's work, but not many of us realize how largely this depends upon the food we eat.

Supposing there to be just money enough in a given family to buy the right kind and quantity of food. Now if this money is not wisely expended, or if after the food has been bought it is spoiled in the cooking, the results will be very serious for the members of that family; they will be under-nourished and they will suffer in clear-headedness, bodily strength, and in the case of children, in bodily development.

Surely the right condition of the body is too important to be left to chance; the best scientific knowledge, the best practical heads should be at its service, and this is the case, indeed, to a large extent in Europe, where the food of the soldiers and of the inmates of public institutions is furnished more or less according to certain rules that have been deduced partly from observation, and partly from scientific experiment.

The application of scientific principles on these lines is not of long standing, for the investigations that have clinched them are all of comparatively recent date. At the end of the last century a beginning was made in France and in Germany in connection with philanthropic efforts to improve the food of the poor, and it was at this time that Count Rumford introduced into the soup kitchens of Munich, the soup that has been named after him. From this time on interest in the subject of foods, both for men and domestic animals, steadily increased, although experimenters were constantly coming to wrong conclusions because the sciences of Organic Chemistry and Physiology, as far as they concerned the subject, were not far enough advanced.

It was only in the early forties that the first experimental agricultural stations were established, but so rapidly have they multiplied that they now number more than a hundred in Europe alone; and in these and in the laboratories of the great universities, analyses have been made of most of the foods used by men and animals, and also tests of the relative flesh and fat producing power of different foods and combinations of foods.

For years the results of these investigations have been applied with profit to the feeding of cattle, but it was a case of threatened wholesale starvation in England that first turned the attention of properly trained persons to a like study of the nourishment of human beings. During our civil war the condition of the cotton spinners in Lancashire and Cheshire, England, became so serious as to make government help necessary to keep them from starving, and in 1862 and 1863 Dr. Edward Smith was commissioned to examine into the the dietetic needs of the distressed operatives.

In his report for 1863 are found tables of the food consumed per week by 634 families, and in spite of the difficulties standing in the way of such an investigation, the foods consumed were classified into tables showing the amounts of the different food principles taken per week by each family.

One of the great practical results following from this investigation was the determination of the minimum amount of each nutritive principle which men, women and children need, to keep them in fair health. The amount of food with which an unemployed man can fight off starvation, and the diseases temporarily incident to it, was found to be represented in 35 ounces of good bread per day, and the necessary amount of wholesome water.

Since the publication of Dr. Smith's report similar inquiries have been instituted by the scientists of other countries, and many analyses have been made of the exact amount and kinds of food eaten by various classes of laborers under the most varied conditions. Professors Voit and Pettenkofer of Munich have even accounted for every particle of food that passed through the body of a man, both while he was at work and while he was idle. They have also noted how much of his own body was consumed when he ate nothing. Finally, a great number of averages have been taken and so-called "standard dietaries" constructed, by which is meant the average amount of each of the chief food principles that keep an average muscle-worker in good condition, when doing average work.

Every one will admit that it is of great importance

for the farmer to know in what proportion he shall lay in hay and other food for the winter feeding of his stock; the animals must thrive, but there must be no waste by furnishing food in the wrong quantities or proportions.

For the housewife, the food question in its relation to her family can be stated in the very same words. It is important that she should economize, but her path will be full of pitfalls if she does not understand in what true economy consists. Most people with a real interest in this subject, have had at some period of their lives certain pet theories as to food. Perhaps they have been at one time convinced that most people ate too much, at another, that meat was the all strengthener, or they may have been afflicted with the vegetarian fad, and whatever their special views have been they have thought that they rested them upon facts. But surely they would never have pinned their faith to one-sided diets if they had rightly comprehended the main facts of nutrition. We believe that if these facts as at present interpreted, and the world's experience in applying them, can be put at the command of the housewife, she can use them to great profit.

We have employed the term "food principles"; what do we mean by it? Everyone knows what is meant by a food, as meat or bread, and everyone knows that the food offered us by our butchers and grocers comes from the animal and vegetable kingdoms. The oxygen we breathe and the water we drink nature furnishes for us directly, so to speak, though unfortunately for many of us, and especially for young children, the former is not thought of as a food. Oxygen aside, it has been found by those who have studied the matter, that all foods contain one or more of five classes of constituents, called "nutritive ingredients" or "food principles." These five principles are:

(1) Water.
(2) Proteids.
(3) Fats.
(4) Carbohydrates.
(5) Salts or mineral constituents.

WATER.

It is important to note that our bodies when full-grown are two-thirds water, and that our food contains from 1 to 94% of it. Considering the scope of this essay, it must be left to take care of itself as a food.

PROTEIDS.

A class of nearly allied bodies is included under this head. The whole class is sometimes called "Albumens."

The housewife is familiar with proteids in such foods as the lean of meat, in eggs and cheese. These contain the principle in various proportions; for example,

Lean of meat has - - - -	15–21 %
Eggs in both white and yolk - -	12.5%
Fresh cows' milk on an average - . -	3.4%
Cheese - - - - - - -	25–30 %
Dried Codfish - - - - - -	30 %

Vegetables are more deficient in proteids though the grains and legumes contain much of it.

Wheat flour has - - -	10 to 12 %
Peas, beans and Lentils have	22.85 to 27.7%

In fresh vegetables we find only from ½ to 3%, excepting green peas and beans in which the proteids reach 5 to 6.5%.

FATS.

Fats are obtained from both the animal and vegetable kingdoms. Those used by us in cookery come mostly from animals, and are known to the housewife as butter, lard and tallow. Vegetable food as a rule, is very poor in fats, containing from 0 to 3% only.

Some of the cereals, like corn and oats contain from 4 to 7% of fats.

CARBOHYDRATES.

The bodies classed as "carbohydrates" are found mainly in vegetables. The housekeeper knows them as starches and sugars.

Under the starches proper are included such things as the starches of grains and seeds, Iceland moss, gums and dextrin.

Milk is one of the few animal products that has more than a very small quantity of carbohydrates. It contains on the average about 4.8% of this principle;—slightly more than of either proteids or fats.

SALTS.

The things that give hardness to our bones, like

calcium phosphate, and the common salt with which we flavor our food, illustrate this class.

FUNCTIONS OF FOOD PRINCIPLES.

To know in what proportion these food principles should be represented in our diet, we must inquire into the part played by each of them in the body. The first and the last principle may be dismissed briefly. The former, water, is the great medium which floats things through the body; the latter, salts, are combined in various ways with the solids and fluids of our foods, and we shall not easily suffer from lack of them.

The other three food principles (let us call them in the following pages the three great food principles), cannot be so summarily dealt with. We might say, briefly and dogmatically, that the proteids are "flesh foods," the fats are "heat foods," the carbohydrates "work foods." To be sure, experimenters are agreed on the main points, but the different schools are still at war on the final explanations and on many details, and it has become more and more evident that we cannot portion off the work of the body in this simple style. Though each of the three great food principles can be said to have a favorite part which it plays better than any other, yet we find that like an actor of varied talents, it has more than one rôle in its repertoire.

FUNCTION OF PROTEIDS.

That this class is indispensable we have the best of proofs. It must be given us in one or another of its forms, for, even if we are not athletes, nearly one half of our body is made up of muscle which is one fifth proteid, and the nitrogen in this proteid can only be furnished by proteid again, since neither fats nor carbohydrates contain any of it; therefore in making up bills of fare, let us remember that growing and working proteid, yes, even idle proteid as Dr. Smith found, needs proteid, and that there is nothing in any of the other food principles that can entirely take its place.

Though we think of proteid mostly as a great body builder and restorer, it can also to some extent furnish fat when it stands in a certain relation to the fats and carbohydrates of our food, and we are assured by experimenters that it also furnishes heat and muscle energy under certain conditions.

In these last two activities, however, it is far excelled by fats and carbohydrates. We shall therefore think of it as the nitrogen-furnisher of our tissues, and also as the grand stimulant among foods, inciting the body, as it does, to burn up more of other kinds.

Scientists, at one time, held the opinion that our muscle energy comes chiefly from proteids. This view has been abandoned, but many a working man still believes that meat is the only kind of food that is of any account; he thinks of fats and starches as quite unimportant comparatively. Now it has been proved over and over again, that we can combine meat with fats and vegetable food in such a proportion that it shall play only its main rôle, viz., that of building and restoring, while these latter furnish the heat and muscle energy needed. Proteid food is such a costly article that it will not do to put it at work which cheaper material can do even better.

FUNCTION OF FATS.

The fats also have more than one office in the body. They can be stored as body fat, or they can be burned and give off heat, and they may also serve as a source of muscular energy, in an indirect manner at least.

FUNCTION OF CARBOHYDRATES.

The Carbohydrate principle furnishes fat to our tissues, and is a source of heat and muscle energy, indeed the chief source of muscle energy in all ordinary diets.

FLAVORINGS.

So far we have had chiefly in mind the real working constituents of food, if we may so speak. But many things cannot be studied or classified in the above way; they must be looked at from another point of view.

Thus, a pinch of pepper, a cup of coffee, a fine, juicy strawberry,—what of these? They may contain all five of the food principles, but who cares for the proteid action or carbohydrate effect of his cup of good coffee at breakfast, or what interest for us has the heating effect of the volatile oil to which the strawberry owes a part of its delicious taste?

Surely the economical housekeeper who would throw out of the list of necessaries all the things that tickle the palate, that rouse the sense of smell, that please the eye and stimulate our tired nerves, just because these things contain but little food, would make a grave mistake. She may know just what cuts of meat to buy, what vegetables are most healthful and economical, but if she does not understand how to "make the mouth water," her labor is largely lost. Especially if she has but little money, should she pay great attention to this subject, for it is the only way to induce the body to take up plain food with relish.

The list of these spices, flavors, harmless drinks and the like, is a long one. Unfortunately, we have no comprehensive word that will include everything of the sort, from a sprig of parsley to a cup of coffee; the German calls them "Genuss-mittel"—"pleasure-giving things."

PROPORTIONS AND AMOUNTS OF FOOD PRINCIPLES.

We have brought our discussion of the three great food principles to the point where we can enquire in what proportions and amounts these should be represented in our diet.

The standard daily dietary that is most frequently cited, and which, perhaps, best represents the food consumption of the average European workman in towns, is that proposed by Prof. Voit. This dietary was made upon the basis of a large number of observed cases. It demands for a man of average size, engaged in average manual labor,

Proteids.*	Fats.	Carbohydrates.
118 gms.	56 gms.	500 gms.

Now it is the opinion of all competent judges, that

*28.34 grams. = 1 oz.

at least one third of this proteid should come from the animal kingdom, and this one third, if given in the form of fresh beef, would be represented by 230 grams of butcher's meat, calculated to consist of

Bone and tendon, - - - - -	18 gms.
Fat, - - - - - - - - -	21 "
Lean, - - - - - - - -	191 "

When we take whole populations into account, we find that little, if any, more meat than this falls to each person per day. Thus the average consumption per day for three great cities is given as follows;

Berlin, - - - - -	135 gms. per cap.
New York, - - - - -	226 " " "
London, - - - - -	274 " " "

Of course these averages include children, but they also include great numbers of the well-to-do, who eat much more meat than their bodies need.

We will add a few more examples of dietaries, some of which are used by the writer in making out the bills of fare given in this essay.

Proteids, gms.	Fats, gms.	Carbohydrates, gms.	
145	100	450	Proposed by Prof. Voit for a man at hard work.
120	56	500	Allowed to German soldiers in garrison.
150	150	500	Proposed by Prof. Atwater for American at hard work.
125	125	450	By the same for American at moderate work.
100	60	400	Proposed by Prof. Voit for a woman.
80	50	320	By the same for children from 7 to 15 years.

We will give an instance of how much below these figures the amount consumed sometimes falls.

Prof. Boehm found that a poor North German family, consisting of a man, wife and a child five years old, had in one week for their food:

Potatoes, - - - - - - -	41 lbs.
Rye flour, - - - - - - -	2½ lbs.
Meat, - - - - - - -	1¾ lbs.
Rice, - - - - - - - -	½ lb.
Rye Bread, - - - - - -	12 lbs.

A very little milk.

Calculating the food principles contained in these amounts, we find that the three individuals daily consumed of:

Proteids,	Fats,	Carbohydrates,
175.5 gms.	41 gms.	1251. gms.

It needs no comment to show how insufficient is this dietary in amount, and how incorrect in proportion.

We have selected Prof. Atwater's dietary for a man at moderate manual labor as the basis of our twelve bills of fare and have taken Voit's standard for women and children.

Our climate is more trying and our people work faster, and we shall do well to allow more fat and meat to our working-man than the foreign dietaries provide. If our man is to get daily one-third of his proteid in the form of animal food, this would be represented by 8 ozs. of butcher's meat (without bone), by from 5 to 5.8 ozs. cheese, or by 8 eggs.

We believe that it is better to go a little high rather than too low with proteid food. As a rule, people who eat enough porteids, and especially enough animal food, are vigorous and have what we call "stamina," and doctors incline to the belief that such people resist disease better because their blood and tissue are less watery than in the case of people who draw their proteids almost entirely from such vegetables as potatoes. But many workingmen in America would be surprised to learn how well health and strength can be maintained on what is, after all, not such a very large amount of meat, provided the rest of the dietary contains enough vegetable proteid and fat.

PRACTICAL APPLICATIONS.

It now remains for us to see whether the economist can get practical help from the foregoing facts about the character of foods and the use that is made of them in the body.

We have seen that we cannot economize in the amount of our food beyond certain limits and yet remain healthy and strong; also that we must not greatly alter the relative proportions in which experience has shown that these foods are best combined. The true field of household economy has, then, certain prescribed limits.

Its scope lies, 1st. In furnishing a certain food principle in its cheap rather than its dear form; for example, the proteid of beef instead of that of chicken, fat of meat instead of butter. 2nd. Having bought foods wisely, in cooking them in such a manner as to bring out their full nutritive value; for instance, making a roast juicy and delicious instead of dry and tasteless. 3d. In learning how to use every scrap of food to advantage, as in soup making, and 4th, if we add to these the art of so flavoring and varying as to make simple materials relish, we have covered the whole field of the household economist, so far as the food question is concerned.

We hope she will find help in the following pages, for it will be part of our task in this essay to examine different articles of food as to their nutritive value, and to recommend such combinations and such methods of cooking as will make the utmost out of a certain sum of money. As to foods, we have in America a large range of choice; staple raw products cost less generally than they do in Europe and the laboring man here has somewhat more money to buy with. The anxious provider, who must feed many mouths on what seems an insufficient sum, may feel assured that he can, without doubt, learn to do better than he now does. In this line we must not disdain to learn lessons wherever we can.

There is an unfortunate prejudice among us against learning of foreign countries. The American workman says indignantly that he does not want to learn how to live on "starvation wages." But the facts, viewed coolly, are just these: the inhabitants of older countries have learned some lessons that we too must soon learn whether we will or no, and to profit by these lessons before we are really obliged to, will in no way lower wages, it will simply help us to get more comfort and pleasure out of our money.

Students of economy, political and domestic, find

no better school than the experience of older countries, and constantly draw lessons from their greater thrift and economy in living. Mrs. Helen Campbell found, among the poor sewing women of New York, that none were skillful in cooking their scanty food excepting only the German and Swiss women. All observing travelers unanimously give this testimony,—"If our American workman knew how to make as much of his large wage as the foreigner does of his small one, he could live in luxury."

But you ask, what are the special lessons to be learned of the foreign housewife? We answer, chiefly self-denial and saving. Do not give up in despair because you have a small income and resign yourself to living meanly, in a hand to mouth fashion. Diligent study of the question and resolute abstention from luxuries will solve the problem, if it can be solved.

We indulge ourselves and our children too much in what tastes good, while all the time we know we have not money enough to buy necessaries. For instance, the consumption of sugar in America was in 1887, 56 lbs. per head, in Germany hardly more than one third that amount. This means a larger consumption of sweetmeats than we can afford and at the same time be well fed otherwise.

We seem, in general, to spend too much money in our country on food compared with what we use in other directions; one great trouble is that we do not know how to save every scrap of food and use it again in some form. For one thing, we have yet to learn the great art of soup making,—and it seems also, of soup eating.

The American housekeeper would say to me: "This is nothing new, for years we've been hearing about soups. We don't like soups!" I only ask, "have you tried them for a considerable length of time, so that you have become skilled in making them, and your family used to their taste?" One fact alone ought to insure for them a good trial; that at least three nations, the French, German and Italian, make daily use of them and have for generations. To take part of our food in this form is an absolute necessity if we are to do the best possible with a certain amount of money.

PRACTICAL DIFFICULTIES.

The practical difficulties in the way of improvement in household cookery are not small. As cook, we have the wife and mother, who has too little time for this very important branch of household work; she has had, perhaps, no good training in the art of cookery (for it is an art), and besides, her kitchen and kitchen utensils are not at all what they should be. Indeed, the qualifications for a given task could not well be further from the ideal.

In Europe families of small means have many helps unknown to us. In the first place, bread is never baked at home, the bakers' bread being both excellent and cheap. It would seem that among us, bakers' bread must shortly improve in quality and decrease in price; either the profits must be too large, or the business not well managed. For instance, in those parts of Germany where white bread is eaten as a staple, it costs a trifle over 3 cents a pound, while flour of average quality costs about the same. In contrast with this, compare the prices of bread and flour in our own country where in no large city is bread quoted at less than 7 cents, while flour costs 3 cents. That is, bread costs in Germany about the same as flour and in America more than twice as much; and yet the German baker is notably a prosperous person!

The foreign housekeeper has still further help from the baker. If she makes a cake or pie, she sends it out to be baked, and pays from one to two cents (the fuel would have cost more); joints of meat and mixed dishes are also sent to be baked for the same price; and before any bakeshop in a German city, at noon on Sunday, can be seen a line of servant girls, each in turn receiving a steaming dish as it is taken from the oven. The soup kitchens (*Volks Küchen*) of various grades are also a great help. The writer has repeatedly had brought from one of them an excellent meat broth (1 pt. for 2 cents), and good cooked vegetables are furnished for a price less than they could be cooked for at home, if one took any account of time and fire.

But such helps are not yet to any great extent available to the American woman; she must wrestle with her own problem at home and solve it as best she can.

THE KITCHEN.

The kitchen of a woman of average means is not the ideal kitchen. It is perhaps too small or not light enough, or it may have still more serious defects, as a bad drain. We must take it as it is, however, requiring only that it contain what is necessary to the end we have in view,—plain cooking for a family of six.

Size of Kitchen. In the cheaper city dwellings the kitchen is small, too small for good ventilation, and for the heavier kinds of work as washing; but for cooking, a very small kitchen can be so arranged as to answer every purpose.

Any one who has seen a ship's kitchen can understand this. The cook as he stands before his range is within reach of all his stores, for rows of drawers and shelves literally line the walls from floor to ceiling, little tables for pastry or cake making are drawn out of the wall and pushed in again when not wanted, and every inch of floor and wall space is used to the best advantage. This cook would tell you that he did not want a larger kitchen; he would only lose time running about in it.

Arrangement. Begin to utilize the wall space. If you have not yet as many shelves as the walls will accommodate, put up more, and especially about and above the stove, so that as you stand at your cooking you can reach salt, pepper and every other flavor that can be used in a soup or stew; cooking spoons and forks and knives, potlids and holders —all these should be at your hand. Let a carpenter fasten into the mortared wall strips of wood that will hold nails and a few shelves, and if the stove is in a niche with wall on two or even three sides of it, all the better. On these nails should hang nearly every implement used in cooking, and on the shelves should be found all spices and flavors; farther back can be placed what is more seldom used. If there are no drawers, never mind, use close tin boxes for as many things as you can; if no closed cupboard for your dishes, hang a curtain before the open shelves.

The nearer your sink is to the stove the better, that is the path your feet must oftenest travel. There must be a table of some sort very near the stove; if it is a movable one, all the better, or it may be a broad shelf with a very strong and safe hinged support under it, letting down when not in use.

I take for granted that the main part of your work is to be done on this stove and table, and that a well stocked pantry, fitted out for the making of pastry and cake and elaborate dishes, is not within your reach any more than the time for making such.

Utensils.

The utensils you need are few, but these few you must have. Consider the value of the food materials that you use; a few burns on an old sauce pan will quite buy a new one. We will speak only of the most important and absolutely necessary utensils.

First, do not use tin; it is cheap, but coal is not, and you will waste a great deal of coal in trying to cook in tin. Brass and copper cooking vessels are to be avoided by one who must economize, as they are expensive and require too much care to keep them free from the poisonous verdigris.

Of chief importance among your utensils is a flat bottomed iron pot with close fitting *iron* lid. Get the smoothest and best, even if it cost double. In this you will roast meat with little fire, cook vegetables, all but peas and beans, cook anything indeed that is not acid. Have two of these, if you can, of different sizes. Next, an iron frying pan, also of the smoothest wrought iron and light; this too should have a close fitting cover. Some people consider iron utensils heavy and old fashioned, but where economy is an object, no other ware is so good and satisfactory. The blue or grey enamelled ware is very nice but will not stand great heat and easily chips and cracks, but you should have one kettle of this ware as it is valuable for cooking fruit and anything acid. You must have a wire gridiron for toasting bread and broiling meat; this you should use for many things which you now cook in the frying pan. The tea-kettle is a matter of course, and a griddle. There is one other utensil not as common, but which deserves to be, viz., a steamer; a simple pot with perforated bottom which will fit tightly into the top of the iron pot, and have a very tightly fitting cover. Its use will be discussed later.

You can hardly do without a number of earthen jugs, glazed with lead-free enamel, especially for cooking and holding milk. Get also a number of wooden spoons; they are cheap and clean, and of convenient shape for stirring. The old fashioned pudding stick of the Yankee kitchen is the earliest form among us, and many people know no other.

Stoves. A good stove is of first importance in a kitchen, but fortunately good stoves have become common. A graver question, however, is the cost of fuel to be burned in them. Of course coal must be the stand-by, and when the stove is heated up as on ironing and baking days, care can be taken to use the fire to its fullest capacity; in winter, dishes can be cooked ahead for several days.

Coal Oil. To cook a single dish or for boiling a tea-kettle a coal oil stove is a saving; it is also invaluable for keeping a pot at a simmering heat,—a thing very difficult to accomplish on a stove.

Charcoal. For the same purpose, and for any steady cooking, and above all for broiling meat, every housekeeper ought to have appliances for burning charcoal; it only needs a grating with a rim 2 or 3 inches high, to let down into the stove hole (a sort of deep spider with a grated bottom). For such purposes, a bushel of hard wood charcoal costing 15 or 20 cents would last a long time. Charcoal is almost the only fuel used in Paris for cooking; indeed, throughout France and in Western Germany it is in very common use.

"Cooking Safe." For "Cooking Safe" as a saver of fuel, see page 44.

PROTEID-CONTAINING FOODS

AND THEIR PREPARATION.

We have already in the Introduction called attention to the importance of this food principle. It is well for us to bear in mind that there are three great classes of Proteids, Albumens proper, Caseins, and and Fibrins, and that in both plants and animals are found representatives of these three classes. Thus, in plant juices and in eggs we have things belonging to the Albumen class; in the curd of sour milk and in the legumine of the pod-covered plants we have examples of caseins; and in the gluten of grains and in the clot whipped out of blood we have examples of fibrins.

ANIMAL FOODS.

Our animal foods contain some other things that the housewife ranks with proteids and we have a few words to say about one of them, viz., gelatine, that nitrogenous substance boiled out of bones and cartilage.

Gelatine, Hist. of

In the history of foods this gelatine, like meat extract, has played a great part. Before the real functions of the food principles were understood it was thought that what could be extracted by water from a piece of meat comprised all in it that was of value to the body; and so it happened that for more than a hundred years after Papin had discovered the method of extracting all the gelatine out of bones (which he did by the aid of that contrivance still known in kitchens as the "Papin Soup Digester") gelatine was considered to be one of the most, if not the most nourishing constituent of meats. In the last decade of the 18th century, and in the early part of this the French made great use of gelatine under the impression that it was a proteid because it yielded nitrogen to the chemist. Improved methods of extracting it were invented, and so general did its use become, especially in the public institutions of Paris, that from 1829–38, two and three quarters million portions of bone-gelatine soup were dealt out to the inmates of a single hospital. But in spite of the opinions of eminent scientists that gelatine soups and gelatine tablets were a perfect substitute for proteids, their consumption decreased; physicians again took hold of the subject, and by the middle of the century opinion had so changed that nearly all, if not all, food value was denied to them. Modern experimentation based on more rational methods has put gelatine in its right place. It is a food, just as much so as is fat, but like fat it cannot play the rôle of proteid although a certain amount taken with fats and carbohydrates will enable the body to get along with a little less proteid. It is even said by Prof. Voit to excel fat in its ability to do half duty for proteid material.

We have thought it well to speak of this because of a sort of superstitious regard in the kitchen for "stock," a survival, one would think. of Papin's time.

A good German housewife was wont to discourse to the writer on the economical virtues of a certain "Frau Doctor" who "always boiled her bones three times" and dwellers in many a household have had their nostrils assailed by the smell of glue, during the sixth hour of bone boiling.

But if the importance of gelatine was and is still exaggerated, this is still more true of the other parts of meat that can be extracted by water.

Sol. Albumen and Extractives. We have seen that hot water coagulates proteid, and once coagulated, it will not dissolve in water, and for this reason the soup generally contains of this valuable principle only the soluble albumen which rose as scum. If the cook has skimmed this off, the soup which she calls strong is strong with flavors rather than with nutritive principles.

To show how very little real food a good tasting meat soup may contain, we will give an analysis made by Prof. König.

Analysis of Soup. He took 1 lb. of beef and about 6½ oz. of veal bones, and treated them, he says, as is usually done in the kitchen to get a pint of good strong soup or bouillon. This contained

Proteids,	Fat,	Extractives,	Salts.
1.19%	1.48%	1.83%	.32%

But where are the albumens that were in the meat to begin with? Many of them are still there in that stringy, sodden mass, the "soup meat," which the cook tells us contains no further value. It consists of cooked connective tissue and albumen; now these are foods and they must be rescued from the garbage barrel, for with the help of the chopping knife and the herb bag we can make them still do proteid duty in our bodies.

Real importance of Soup.

If we do not overvalue either the gelatine or the flavoring matters in our meat soups, nor throw away the meat out of which they are made, we shall begin to make soups on the right basis, that is an understanding of the real value of the materials we are working with, and we shall use meat for our soups less often than we now do perhaps, considering its high price and our greater need of it cooked in other ways. Soups should not be regarded as a luxury, neither as the last resort of poverty, but as a necessary part of a dinner, just as they are now used by all classes in Europe; but they need not be made of good cuts of meat, nor indeed, of meat at all.

Proteid as we buy it.

We will now direct our attention to the proteid as we buy it.

We cannot here take up the chemical composition and exact nutritive value of every kind of meat to be bought at the butcher's stall, the fish market and the poultry stand. But we must note a few points of importance.

Butchers' meat.

We know that butchers' meat contains from 50% to 78% of water, according to the quality of the piece and the kind of animal. Most people in buying meat think first of the red part; they may know that it is advantageous to buy meat that is streaked with fat, but they hardly realize how wise it is to do so. As a rule, fat takes the place of water. Let us consult tables of analyses for the amounts of water, proteids and nitrogenous extractives, fats and salts contained in lean pieces and in pieces streaked with fat. In Prof. König's valuable treatise on Foods we find such analyses, carefully collected and sifted out of a large amount of material;

Prof. König's Analyses of Meat.

samples of neck, tenderloin, shoulder, hind-quarter and so on, just as bought at the butchers', were analyzed after being freed from adherent *lump* fat, and the average composition of all the different cuts was as follows:—

Fat and lean ox compared.

	Water	Nitrogenous Substances	Fat
	%	%	%
From a very fat ox....	55.42	17.19	26.38
From a medium fat ox	72.25	20.91	5.19
From a lean ox	76.71	20.78	1.50

These tables illustrate how wise it is to buy meat from a very fat animal. They show that a pound of meat from a fat ox may have more than 20% less water than a corresponding piece from a lean one; of course such a piece may contain from 3 to 4% less proteid, but to compensate for this, it will have 25% more fat.

Let us give another table which illustrates that pieces like tenderloin are not the richest in proteids and fats, though they do have the finest flavor. It may help to console those whose purses do not allow them to buy these expensive cuts.

Dif. part of ox compared	Water	Nitrogenous Substances	Fat
	%	%	%
Neck	73.5	19.5	5.8
Shoulder	50.5	14.5	34.
Tenderloin	63.4	18.8	16.7
Hind-quarter	55.05	20.81	23.32

In this case the difference between shoulder and tenderloin as to the amount of water contained in each is striking. In the case of *medium* fat and lean animals, poor and good pieces approach each other more nearly in composition.

We regret that the scope of this essay will not allow us to give drawings and full illustrations of the different parts of an animal, with advice in detail as to what to buy. We are glad to mention in this connection a former prize essay—"Healthy Homes and Foods for the Working Classes"—which gives much information needed by the housekeeper as to the qualities and comparative value of the meat from different animals, of milk and milk products.

Some meats compared.

Of butchers' meat beef must always be considered the most economical, its choice being governed by facts just stated. Fat mutton also ranks high.

Pork.

Pork. Say what we may against pork, it is a most valuable kind of meat, especially for the poor man, and the laws governing its slaughter and sale should be so stringent as to protect him. The great importance of salt pork and bacon we have considered under "Fats."

It is of little use to give rules about buying this meat; we must generally take what the butcher furnishes, but at least we can cook it well, never eating it raw even when well dried and smoked.

Fish.

Fish. From the standpoint of the economist fish is worthy of especial mention; nature does the feeding, we have only to pay for the catching. In the season when it is best and cheapest, fresh fish should be used freely. We have only to remind the housewife that she loses ⅓ to ¼ of the weight of a fish in bones and head.

Salted and smoked fish.

Salted and smoked fish is of great importance as food, and not alone for people living on the sea-coast. Salted cod contains, according to König's tables, 30% of Proteids, and this fact, together with its low price, fully justifies its popularity with all economical people.

Other salted and preserved fish, as for instance, the herring, give variety in the diet of many a poor family.

LIVER, HEART, ETC.

Internal Organs.

Of the internal organs of animals generally considered eatable, we really appreciate only the liver. The lungs, brains, kidneys, heart, and the stomach prepared as tripe, are good food and they are often sold very cheap in country towns. The head of most animals, as of the calf, is excellent for soups and other dishes, and in the country it is often given away.

EGGS.

Eggs compared with meats as a food.

To get an idea of the comparative value of eggs as a food let us compare them with medium fat beef.

	Water %	Proteids %	Fat %
Medium fat beef has..	72.5	21.	5.5
Eggs have............	74.5	12.5	12.

We see that while the water is nearly the same in both, the meat has the advantage in proteids and the eggs the advantage in fat, this fat, moreover, being of very fine quality.

Take eggs at their cheapest, as in April when they often sell at 15 cents a dozen, that would be 12½ cents a pound, 10 eggs of average size weighing a pound. They could then be considered cheaper than the highest priced cuts of meat, but still much dearer than the cheaper parts, flank, neck and brisket, at 8 cents. So that even at this low price, they are somewhat of a luxury to the man who must get his proteid and fat in their cheapest form.

And when we consider that only for a short time in the year is the price so low,—eggs being on an average quoted at 25 to 30 cents, the showing for them as a proteid rival of meat is poor indeed. Except in the Spring the economically inclined must be sparing of their use even in dessert dishes. When housekeepers say, as I have heard them, that eggs at 25 cents a dozen are cheaper than meat, they must be speaking in comparison with very high priced meats.

CHEESE.

Cheese (its food value.)

In America, cheese is regarded more as a luxury than as a staple article of food, and yet 1 lb. of cheese is equal in food value to more than 2 lbs. of meat, it being very rich in both fat and proteids. Considering this, its price is very low and it ought to be a treasure to the poor man and do good service in replacing sometimes the more expensive meat.

Use of cheese abroad. Its food value is fully recognized abroad. For the Swiss peasant it is a staple second only to bread, while the use of it in Italy and in Germany is extensive. The writer once spent several weeks in the house of a large farmer on the slope of Mt. Pilatus in Switzerland, and observed daily the food given to the harvesters; the luncheon sent twice a day to the fields consisted of a quarter section of the grayish skim cheese, accompanied with bread. I was told that the poor people in the region ate scarcely any meat, using cheese in its stead.

The writer has also observed the use of cheese in Germany. Every locality has its special variety of the soft kind made of sour milk, and great amounts of the Swiss, both skim and full milk, cheese are consumed. It is generally eaten uncooked, but also as an addition to cooked food in a great variety of dishes.

Digestibility of cheese. There is no doubt of the food value of cheese, but there does seem to be some question as to its digestibility. When we come to inquire into this point, we find that thorough experiments have been made by German scientists; Dr. Rübner, a pupil of Voit, gives the result of experiments on himself. He found that he could not consume much of it alone, but with milk he took easily 200 grams, or nearly ½ lb., and only when he took as high as 517 grams or over a pound daily, was it less completely digested than meat. Prof. König says, that in the amounts in which it is generally eaten, 125 to 250 grams daily (¼ to ½ lb.), it is as well digested as meat or eggs. The extensive use of it abroad would seem to be some guarantee for the digestibility of the foreign varieties at least.

American cheeses have in general a sharper flavor than the foreign, still it is probable that well mixed with other food, enough could be taken many a time, to give a man his needed daily quantity of animal proteid,—between six and seven ounces,—and this is a matter of great importance from an economical point of view.

METHODS OF COOKING MEAT.

Why cook. And first—why do we cook it at all? In the animal as well as in the vegetable world some foods are all ready for our digestion, as milk. Raw eggs too, are perfectly digestible and are often given to invalids. We hear, of "Raw meat cures," and it has been found that tender and juicy raw meat, if chopped fine to break the connective tissue, is well digested.

But raw meat does not taste good to most of us, while the delicious flavor and odor of a broiled steak make it very acceptable to the palate, and we must believe to the stomach also. We "bring out the flavor," as we say, by cooking; what else do we do? Let us examine for a moment a piece of meat with reference to the effect heat has upon it.

Structure of meat. The red part is made up of, first, very tiny sausage-like bags, or muscle fibres as they are called, and in these is contained the precious proteid matter, flavors and salts all mixed together with water into a sort of jelly; second, these muscle fibres are bound together by strands of connective tissue, as that white stringy mass is called, in which the fat and blood vessels are lodged; this is also of food value, but inferior to the fibres. Third, dissolved in the juices floating between the fibres and strands, there is also a proteid called soluble albumen. The little bags of proteid, when we can get at them, are as digestible in our stomachs as is the white of egg, though, like the egg again, their flavor is improved by slight cooking. But, as we have seen, they are imprisoned in the connective tissue, somewhat, we may say, as are the starch grains of the potato in the cellulose.

Softening connective tissue. This connective tissue we can soften by heat, thereby turning it into a sort of gelatine, but unfortunately, unless the meat is very tender, this requires a longer application of heat than is needed to cook the delicate albumen all full of flavors too easily lost. To soften the connective tissue without overcooking the albumen, is one of the problems of meat cookery.

The next question is, how do our methods of cooking meet these requirements?

COOKING MEAT IN WATER.

1st. Method. Put a piece of lean meat into cold water, heat it very slowly and watch the effect. The water becomes slightly red, then cloudy, and as the heat increases, yellowish in color, and finally it clears, sending a scum to the surface. If we examine this scum, we find that the water has soaked out much soluble albumen and a large proportion of the salts of the meat as well as other substantives called extractives; and now the odor of the boiling meat begins to fill the kitchen. The longer and slower the warming process, the more of all these things we shall extract, and the meat when taken out will be in just that proportion poor.

Soup making. This is the process known as soup making,—very simple, if we care nothing for the piece of meat but to soak out of it all the food and flavors possible. After some hours of cooking we find it shrunken, gray and tasteless. A dog if fed on that alone could not live many days. However, as we have before said, we are not to conclude, that it contains no more nutriment, but the stomach rejects it now that it is separated from all the flavoring matters.

2nd Method. Now put a piece of meat into boiling water and continue the boiling. The surface of the meat suddenly whitens and a little scum rises on the water, though very little compared with what we saw in the former method. We have coagulated the albumen contained in all the little cells in the surface of the meat, and the soluble albumen, flavoring matters and salts cannot get out; the sealing up is not quite perfect, enough escaping into the water to make it a weak soup, but it is a good method of cooking a large piece if properly completed from this point. But if we *go on* boiling our meat, that is, keeping the temperature at 212°, we shall overcook the albumen in the outer layers before that in the center is coagulated. By overcooking, we mean making it horny and flavorless, as we do the white of an egg if we cook it in the old-fashioned way, by dropping into boiling water and keeping it at that heat. Having seared the outside of the meat to keep the juices in, we must lower the temperature. The albumen coagulates at between 160° and 170°, but the water in the kettle may be a little above this, as it must constantly transfer heat to the interior of the meat. The general rule is that it should "babble" or "simmer" only, and if the cook can do no better she must follow these indications. That the true temperature for cooking meat is below the boiling point, many an intelligent housekeeper knows, but how is she to know when the water is at 170°? Here we come upon the weakest point in household cookery; various degrees of heat have different effects on the foods we cook, but of only one temperature is the housekeeper certain—that of boiling water.

For the use of the thermometer and the heat saver see pages 43 and 44.

But to return; is there no way of cooking that will keep in the meat all these flavors and salts and albumens, just as nature mixed them? Yes, there are three ways,—frying in fat, baking in an oven, and broiling over coals.

Frying in fat.

We will examine the first. If we plunge a thin piece of meat, as a cutlet coated with egg and breadcrumbs, into boiling fat, the albumen in the surface or rather in that of the egg surrounding it is coagulated as in boiling, but this time the outer rind preserves the juices still better because the fat will not mix with them as will water. Everyone knows how an oyster cooked in this way retains its juices.

Baking meat.

When we bake a piece of meat in the oven, we start in the same way; we sear the outside in fat, turning the roast about in a small quantity of fat made hot in a kettle; we then transfer it, still in the kettle or pan, to a hot oven where the process of cooking is completed, but at short intervals we moisten the surface with the fat in the pan. If we did not baste the roast, we would find a thick layer of grey, tasteless meat inside the outer brown crust, and indeed the whole piece would dry long before the center of our roast had reached the coagulating point; we baste, in order to keep in the juices which, as we know, will not mix with the fat, and also that only a mild degree of heat, not exceeding the coagulating point of proteids, may be transmitted to the interior. In the intervals of our basting, some water is driven out of the meat and evaporated into steam, and the high heat of the oven expends itself in evaporating this, in heating the basting fat, and perhaps (if it reach so high a temperature) in decomposing part of it, and in changing the chemical character of small quantities of extractives, thus making the meat "tasty," and so it happens that only a mild degree of heat is passed into the center of the piece. We would hardly believe that the inside of a roast, with its light pink color, registers only 160° by the thermometer, yet this can be proved by anyone with a long chemist's thermometer.

Although some of the water of our meat has evaporated, the extractives and salts are retained to a larger extent than in boiling, as we shall see by the table given later.

Broiling. In broiling, the principle applied is exactly the same as in baking, the cooking being done by the medium of heated air. The dry heat of the coals affects the outer layer of the meat, as does the hot air of the oven. In both these methods, just as in boiling, we try to hold the temperature of our cooking medium just high enough to keep the heat traveling toward the interior of the meat.

We have now learned to cook the albumen enough and not too much and to keep the flavors of our meat; what about the connective tissue, and how has that fared with our different modes of cooking?

Tender meat.

If our meat is cut from the tenderer parts of an animal of the right age, well fed and fattened, and if it has been kept long enough after killing, the connective tissue will soften into eatable condition in the length of time required to cook the albumen by the methods described. Such meat, so cooked, will always be tender and full of flavor.

Tough meat.

But if the meat is cut from the tougher parts, or from an old or ill-fattened animal, or cooked too soon after killing, the connective tissue will not soften in that time; we must continue the application of heat till this tissue softens.

Methods compared: 1st, as to quality of meat.

Therefore, what method of cooking we shall use, depends on the quality of the meat we have. Trimmings and tough portions we will make into soup, expecting to chop the tasteless meat next day and add other flavors to make it palatable. Somewhat better pieces, but still requiring long cooking to soften the connective tissue, may be made into a stew or ragout; or if the piece is large and compact, boiled in water; but meat that is tender and juicy (and for improving tough meat see page 45) should be boiled, baked or broiled, choosing oftenest the last two methods, because of the more perfect retention of the juices and the fine flavor given to the outer layer.

2d, as to economy. We are told that baking or broiling is a very wasteful way of cooking meat; that if we would be truly economical we would always boil or stew, using our meat or its juices to flavor vegetables. From this we must dissent for it would condemn us to such a monotony as would be unendurable even to the poor. Better sometimes a smaller piece of broiled or baked meat with its delicious and stimulating flavor, and make our soup of vegetables and season it with herbs. Besides, according to the scientists, baking and broiling are *not* wasteful methods. I quote from a table of Prof. König's, wherein are given the results of analysis of beef raw, after boiling and after "*braten.*" Raw, it contained .86% extractives (nitrogenous bodies mostly; very important as giving the stimulating smell and taste) and 1.23% salts.

	Extractives	Salts
Raw	.86%	1.23%
After boiling	.40%	1.15%
After "*braten*"	.72%	1.45%

The advantage is seen to be in favor of "*braten*" both in regard to extractives and salts. The loss of water was nearly the same in both cases. As for the fat lost in broiling a beef steak, that is indeed a loss, but one to be made up in some measure by the smaller quantity of fuel necessary to cook the meat. The loss of this fat need not be made so much of, until we have learned to do better in many other still more important directions.

The philosophy of cooking meat according to the different methods has been treated, and we will now give a few additional directions as to carrying out these methods.

SOUP MAKING.

Materials for Soup making. Lean meat of any sort, beef best; fresh, better than that long kept; bones of next value, especially the spongy rib bones and vertebrae. Saw and chop the bones into little pieces,—cut the meat small. Soft water is better than hard.

Method of making. Keep a kettle, if possible, for this purpose alone, and add to it all bits of meat and bones as they accumulate. Put the meat into cold water, let it stand some hours if possible, heat very gradually and keep *simmering*. Two hours or less brings out all the flavors of the meat, but a much longer time is necessary to get all the nutriment from the bones.

Skimming. Do not remove the scum; it contains the albumen of the soup, and nothing objectionable if the meat was well cleaned.

An hour before the soup is served add flavors; onions and carrots are the best, celery, summer savory, and parsley next. Use others, as cloves, nutmeg, bay leaf, etc., only occasionally. Add salt and pepper just before serving.

When done, strain and skim off all fat (better if

left to stand till next day, the fat removed and the soup simply rewarmed), and make such additions as you wish.

[We prefer our soups with the fat removed, but the laboring people of Europe with their hardy stomachs find a soup much better if covered with "eyes."]

These rules apply to all meat soups. Mutton makes a strong and nutritious soup, veal a delicate soup. An excellent soup is made from a calf's head.

BOILING.

To boil meat. Put the meat into boiling water, bring quickly again to a boil and keep so for 10 minutes, then lower the temperature (as see page 35), and so keep it till the meat in the center has reached 160°–170°, or has changed in color from bluish to red, our usual test. For use of the "Cooking Safe" for this purpose, see page 44. Braising, "a la mode", kettle roasts, &c., are but modifications of this method.

To make meat stews. This is a combination of soup making and boiling. Use inferior parts, cut in pieces and cook, at 170° if possible, till tender. Half an hour before serving, season in any way you wish. See page 47.

FRYING IN FAT.

How to prepare Suet in which to fry meat. Lard if used for this purpose should be tried out at home, but beef fat is cheaper and if nicely prepared no one can object to the taste.

Cut the fresh suet in pieces, and cover with cold water; let it stand a day, changing the water once in the time. This takes out the peculiar tallowy taste. Now put it in an iron kettle, with a half teacup of milk to each pound of suet, and let it cook very slowly till the fat is clear, and light brown in color, and till the sound of the cooking has ceased. The pieces may be loosened from the bottom with a spoon, but it is not to be stirred; if it burns the taste is ruined. Now let it stand and partly cool, then pour off into cups to become cold; it smells as sweet as butter and can in many cases be used instead of it. The fat left still in the pieces may be pressed out for less particular uses.

Any clean fat, even mutton, has its uses in cookery, and should be tried out and kept nicely.

Oils for use in frying. There are oils now sold which but for prejudice we would always use. *Pure* cotton seed oil is a fine oil with a delicate flavor; rape seed oil, which is used extensively abroad for this purpose, is also a pure vegetable oil, but somewhat rank in flavor. It is treated thus: a raw potato is cut up and put into the kettle, heating with the oil and cooking till it is brown, it is then taken out and the oil used like lard. The potato has absorbed the rank flavor.

Thin pieces of meat, like cutlets and chops, are coated with beaten egg and bread crumbs and cooked in boiling fat for 5–10 minutes, according to the kind of meat.

To bake meat. Make some beef fat hot in an iron pan or broad kettle. Put the meat into it, and with a fork stuck into the *fat* part, turn it rapidly till it is on all sides a fine brown, then put it into a hot oven (about 340° F.), elevating it above the pan on a meat rack, or a few iron rods. Now comes the process called basting; in five minutes or less you will find that the top of the meat has dried, and you must now dip, with a spoon, the hot fat from the pan over the top. Do this every few minutes adding *no water* to the pan; you will find your meat well cooked in from 12–15 minutes to the pound. It is done when it has lost, in the middle, the blue color, and become a fine red. Only salt and pepper should be used to season such a roast, and must be added when the meat is half done; if earlier, it toughens the fibres.

Basting.

To broil meat.

But when fuel is expensive, or in summer when a hot fire is a nuisance, the perfectly cooked meat can also be obtained by broiling; the management of the fire is the only trouble. We are told that a beefsteak for broiling should be cut ¾ of an inch thick, and put over a hot fire of coal or charcoal; quite right, but when it has browned quickly, as it should, and been turned and browned on the other side, it yet remains raw in the middle and if left longer, the surface burns. This is the experience of the novice, who has yet to learn two things; first, that immediately after the first browning, the fire must decrease in heat, or the meat be brought further away, so that the steak may cook 10–12 minutes without burning—less time will not cook it nicely in the middle; and second, that like baked meat, the surface must be kept moist with hot fat. Before your steak is put over (unless it be very well streaked with fat), cover both sides with melted suet, and afterwards, as it dries, spread on a little butter or beef fat. Have ready in a hot platter a few spoonsful of water in which the bones cut from the steak have been boiling, also salt and pepper. When the steak is done, lay it in the platter and keep it hot for five minutes, turning it once in the time; thus you will have both good steak and good gravy.

Use of charcoal. Professional cooks always use charcoal for broiling, and its advantages are great. As described on page 21 it needs only a simple contrivance, easily adjusted to any stove; a handful will broil a pound of steak, and the cooking of the rest of the dinner can go on without interference.

USE OF THE THERMOMETER IN COOKING MEAT.

To cook meat at a temperature of between 150° and 160° F., is no easy matter with the usual kitchen appliances. Even over an easily regulated heater, as a gas or coal oil flame, how are we to know that temperature when it is reached? The writer, knowing of no thermometer arranged for use in a kitchen, constructed a simple one after the model of those used in laboratories. A thermometer tube registering 300° Celsius was simply fastened into a cork, the bulb projecting below and protected by a short cylinder of wood. This floated on the water and made it easy to cook at any given temperature. This thermometer was also hung in a light wire frame and used for testing the heat of an oven.

THE HEAT SAVER.

It is a part of common information that the inhabitants of northern countries make extensive use of non-conducting substances, like wool, for preventing the escape of heat from a vessel in which cooking is going on. It is strange that we do not make more use of such appliances, for they have often been described and illustrated; it is probably because they are not found ready-made, and with a complete list of directions for use. The writer made and used a cooker of this sort, and after considerable modification and experiment it became a very useful thing in the kitchen. If you wish to cook meat at the proper temperature, this contrivance makes it possible to do so, and is also very saving of fuel.

Directions for making Heat Saver. Take a packing box measuring, say, 2 feet each way and cover the bottom with a layer of packed wool 4 to 6 inches thick; set into the middle of this another box or a cylinder of sheet iron and fill the space between the two with a layer of wool, 4 to 6 inches thick and closely packed. Into the inner compartment put your kettle of meat or vegetables already brought to the boiling point and having a tightly fitting cover, and over this press a thick pillow or woolen blanket. Then fasten down tight over all, the lid of your box. As the heat in the water must finish the cooking already begun, its amount must be rightly proportioned to the amount of food to be cooked, *e. g.*, two quarts of water to 1½ lbs. beef rib, were used. The water was brought to the boiling point, the meat placed in it and allowed to boil for five minutes, the pot was then tightly covered, placed in the box and allowed to remain three hours. At the end of that time the meat was tender.

TO MAKE MEAT TENDER.

To make meat tender.

It is well known that meat must be kept some time after killing to make it tender. In winter, a large piece of beef or mutton will keep for six weeks if hung in a dry, cool place. Indeed, this is the time allowed in England for the Christmas "shoulder of mutton," and every few days it is rubbed over with salt and vinegar. In summer, unless the butcher will keep the meat for you, you must resort to other means.

A tough piece of meat may be laid in not too strong vinegar for 3 or 4 days in summer and twice as long in winter, adding to the vinegar such spices as you may like. To soften a tough steak pour a few spoonfuls of vinegar on and let stand for twelve or twenty-four hours. This method has been long recommended and is to some extent used among us; the foreign cook employs sour milk for the same purpose and with even greater success, but this must be changed every day and at the end of the time well washed from the meat.

We cannot too strongly urge that the housekeeper, especially if she be straightened in means, should become used to these methods and practice them occasionally. She does not want to confine herself to soups and stews and she cannot buy "porter-house" steak at 20 or 25 cents a pound, but she can buy "round" at half that price, and after a little experiment can make it tender for boiling, roasting or broiling by one of these methods. In winter, she should buy a supply of meat ahead and keep it until it grows tender.

RECIPES FOR COOKING MEATS.

The methods of cooking meat having been treated and mention made of the .parts adapted to each, it remains only to give practical hints as to making and varying dishes.

BEEF.

Boiled, roast and broiled beef have been sufficiently dwelt upon. See pages 40–43.

Stews and Ragouts. No mode of cooking meat has so many variations; the flavor of the meat being used to season vegetables of every sort, also doughs, as in dumplings, or in the crust of meat pie. For making meat stews see page 40.

With potatoes. One-half hour before the meat is done lay on top of it peeled potatoes, all of the same size, and serve when done with the meat and gravy.

Meat pie. When the meat is cooked tender, thicken the gravy and pour all into a pie or pudding dish. Cover with a common pie crust or one of mashed potatoes, and bake ½ hour.

You may also mix sliced raw potatoes with the stew, in layers.

Potato Crust. 4 cup mashed potatoes, 1 egg, 2 tablespoons butter, 1 cup of milk, salt. Beat together till smooth, and then work in enough flour so that you can roll it out. It should be ½ in. thick, and as soft as you can handle.

With tomatoes. Add to meat when tender, 1 qt. tomatoes to 2 lbs. meat. Thicken with flour and stew 5 minutes.

Flavors for stews. Stews are variously flavored; onion, salt and pepper, are always in place. A little lemon juice added as it is served gives a delicious flavor, or even a tablespoon of vinegar may be used. Any herbs, a piece of carrot, a clove or bit of garlic, may be used for variety. Catsup is also good as a flavor.

Corned Beef. Wash it well, put into plenty of cold water and bring slowly to the simmering point. Cook 3 to 4 hours.

Turnips or cabbage are often eaten with corn beef. They should not be boiled with the meat but in a separate pot.

Beef Liver. If from a good animal, beef liver is often as tender as calf's liver.

Broiled. This is the best method. Soak an hour in cold water, wipe dry, slice and dip in melted beef fat. Broil *slowly* (see page 42) till thoroughly done; then salt and butter.

Fried. When prepared as above, the slices of liver may be fried in a pan with a little beef fat. This gives an opportunity for more flavors, as onion may be fried with it, a little vinegar added to the juices that fry out, then thickened and used as gravy.

Baked. If liver is not quite tender it can be made into a stew, or it may be chopped fine, mixed with bread crumbs and egg and baked ½ hour.

Beef's Heart. If fire is no object, you may boil a beef's heart, it will take all day. Put into cold water and bring slowly to the simmering point and keep it there. Next day it may be stuffed with well seasoned bread crumbs and baked ¾ hour.

Tripe. Cut in strips, soak in salt and vinegar ½ day, wipe dry and fry in hot lard. It may also be stewed.

RECOOKING BEEF.

(A.) Boiled, baked or broiled beef which is tender and full of flavor.

To serve roast beef a second time.

Roast beef re-served. Heat the gravy, put the roast in it. After trimming it into shape again, cover closely and put into a hot oven for ten minutes or less according to size of piece.

Or, cut in slices and lay in hot gravy only long enough to heat them through.

Hash. Being full of flavor such meat may be chopped and mixed with from ⅓ to ½ as much chopped or mashed potatoes, bread crumbs or boiled rice. These mixtures may be warmed as hash, or made into cakes or balls to be fried on a griddle or in boiling fat.

Mix the chopped meat with the potatoes, bread-crumbs or rice as above, add salt and pepper and make quite moist with water or soup. Put a good piece of butter or of beef fat into a spider, and when it is hot, put in the hash. Cover and let it steam, then remove cover and let it dry out while a brown crust forms on the bottom. *Or*, stir till hot and dish immediately.

Hash balls. Make not quite as moist as for hash, form into little cakes, dust with flour, and fry to a nice brown in a little beef dripping on a griddle. *Or*, egg and bread crumb the balls, and fry in boiling fat.

(B.) RECOOKING SOUP MEAT.

This meat, though made tender by long cooking, has given much of its flavor to the soup. It has not, to the same degree, however, lost its nutritive value; if we can make it *taste* good again, both palate and stomach will approve it.

It will not do to mix this meat with neutral substances like potatoes and bread; it needs addition rather than subtraction.

In any case, first chop the meat very fine.

Pressed soup meat. Season the chopped beef well with salt and pepper, and some other addition, as celery salt or nutmeg, or some of the sweet herbs. Moisten with soup or stock, pack in a square, deep tin and place in the oven for a short time. To be sliced cold, or warmed as a meat hash to be served on toast.

Meat Croquettes. When so good a dish as this can be made out of soup meat, it is worth a little trouble.

Ingredients. 2 cups of the chopped beef, 1 tablespoon butter, 1 tablespoon flour, 1 egg, ½ a lemon or 1 tablespoon vinegar, a few gratings of nutmeg and ½ cup of stock or milk.

Cook the flour in the butter and add the stock or milk and seasoning, then the beef, and cook, stirring all the time till the mass cleaves from the side of the kettle. Let it get cold, then make into little egg shaped balls, let them dry a little, roll in beaten egg and bread crumbs and fry in boiling fat.

To vary—add ⅓ as much chopped salt or fresh pork as you have meat.

VEAL.

This meat takes other flavors well and is used by cooks for all manner of fancy dishes. It is lacking in fat and for that reason easily dries in cooking; an addition of pork is always an advantage to the taste. It must be always well cooked, never rare.

Roast Veal. This may be a piece cut from loin, breast or shoulder, or a rib piece. Roast like beef (see page 35), allowing twice as long, or 1½–2 hours, for any piece under 4 lbs.

Broiled veal chops. Cutlets, chops and steaks are broiled like beef, but slower and twice as long and must be buttered and floured to prevent drying. Should be served with a tomato or onion sauce.

Veal Stew. Cook like beef stew, see page 46. It may be varied in the same way, and is generally more highly seasoned. Especially good as pot-pie. Salt pork should be added to it.

Liver, Sweetbreads and Heart. Veal liver, sweetbreads and heart are all tender and excellent, but high priced, especially the sweetbreads. Liver and heart are prepared like the same parts in beef (see page 47), but the heart cooks tender in two hours. This latter is an excellent dish, do not soak it—stuff with well seasoned bread crumbs and bake, basting well.

MUTTON AND LAMB.

Mutton and Lamb.

The quality of mutton is so varying that when cooked the dish is often a disappointment. The influence of long keeping or "hanging" upon it is even more beneficial than upon beef.

Mutton Fat.

Fat of Mutton. Some cooks trim away every bit of fat from mutton. It is perfectly wholesome, but sometimes gets a taste from coming in contact with the hide or hair of the animal; hence the prejudice. Scrape the outside of the meat well, pulling off the dried skin and cutting away the dark ends.

Pieces to roast.

Unlike beef, other pieces besides the rib are good for roasting; the loin and haunch are most economical, the shoulder next, the leg next. Roast like beef, see page 35.

Unless the meat is first class, do not roast, but boil it. The leg is oftenest used for this purpose.

To boil mutton.

Simmer about 12 minutes to the pound; that is the rule, but very frequently the meat when it comes on the table, will be tough, owing entirely to the difference in the quality of the meat. Such meat must be boiled twice as long, or is better cooked in a stew.

Mutton chops.

The chop is oftenest broiled and is a famous dish. Cut ¾ in. thick, and broil rare like beef.

Chops and cutlets are excellent fried in fat. See page 40.

Mutton stew. This is the most economical and perhaps the most satisfactory of all mutton dishes. The inferior parts, as the neck, are as good as any for this purpose. Proceed exactly as with beef stew.

A good stew is made from sheep's kidneys.

Sheep tongues. These may be mentioned because sometimes thrown away or sold very cheap. Clean well, and simmer 1½ hours, with a little pork and onion. Add to the gravy 1 tablespoon of vinegar.

All these recipes for mutton apply to the cooking of lamb; remembering however, that lamb, like veal, must be thoroughly cooked.

PORK.

Pork does not need to be kept in order to be tender, that is one of its great recommendations to the housekeeper. It is also easily cooked and we may lay aside some of the precautions we use regarding beef: The lean of fresh pork however, is apt to dry in cooking.

Roasting pieces. The leg, the loin and the chine are good roasting pieces as well as the rib. Pork is so rich in flavor that it seasons finely a bread crumb dressing, to which add a little sage and vinegar or chopped pickles. Bake separately, and lay around it when served. Or better, though more trouble, make holes in the roast and force the stuffing in.

Put directly into a hot oven in a pan containing some hot fat, and baste very frequently till done. Allow at least 20 minutes to the pound.

Steaks and chops. Steaks and chops are broiled, but the surface must be kept well moistened with butter or beef fat, or they will be dry and tasteless.

Stew of pork. Fresh pork is seldom boiled and it is too fat for a stew, though the lean may be selected and cooked like beef stew. It makes also an excellent potpie, or meat pie. See page 46.

Pig's Liver. Pig's liver is good cooked like beef's liver, and is cheaper. See page 47.

Pork Sausage. The cooking of this is very simple. Fry brown in a frying pan on the stove, or better, set the pan in a hot oven, you will then avoid the sputtering of the fat.

HAM, SALT PORK AND BACON.

Ham may be cooked in any way in which fresh pork is cooked. It may be cut in ½ in. slices, or thinner, and broiled or fried lightly in a pan. If long cooked it becomes tough and dry. If too salt for this, it may be soaked a half hour in warm water.

A large piece of ham is best boiled. If very salt, soak it in cold water for 24 hours, then put into cold water, bring slowly to a boil, and simmer half a day if the ham is of good size. A ham may also be baked.

Dishes from cold ham. So highly flavored a meat can be used in numberless ways, especially combined with vegetables and bread.

Sandwiches. Chop ½ lb. fine, season with mustard, pepper and 1 tablespoon vinegar. Spread between slices of buttered bread.

Ham cakes. Take 1 cup finely chopped boiled ham, 2 cups of breadcrumbs, 2 eggs, pepper and salt, and enough milk to make quite moist.

To use. 1st. Fry on a griddle in small spoonfuls, and turn as pancakes.

2d. Use mashed potatoes instead of breadcrumbs, and fry as above.

Croquettes. 3d. Take either of the above mixtures, using, however, little or no milk, make into little balls and after rolling in egg and breadcrumbs, fry in boiling fat.

With eggs. 4th. With eggs. Put either of these mixtures into a baking dish; smooth the surface and make little hollows in it with the bowl of a spoon. Put in the oven till hot, then break an egg into each depression, and return to the oven till the eggs are set.

Broiled Salt Pork and Bacon After slicing thin, freshen salt pork by laying in cold water over night or ½ hour in warm water. Broil till transparent and a delicate brown in color. Broil bacon without freshening.

Fried. Less delicate than broiled, but much more economical, because saving the fat. Fry only till transparent. Salt pork must be first freshened. To make milk gravy of the fat, see "meat and vegetable sauces," page 73.

Both salt pork and bacon are boiled with vegetables.

Bacon or Pork and Cabbage. This is a favorite mixture, and if the cabbage is only boiled half an hour and not in the same pot with the pork, it is not an indigestible dish. Put the pork into cold water, bring slowly to a boil and simmer from ½ to 2 hours, according to size of piece.

Pork and Peas. Cook 1 qt. dried peas according to directions for pea soup, page 117. Boil pork with the peas during the last hour, or after parboiling, bake like pork and beans.

Pork and Beans. Cook 1 qt. beans according to soup recipe, page 117. Parboil 1 lb. salt side pork, score the skin in squares, half bury in the beans and bake 2 hours, or till a nice brown.

Pork and Potatoes. Slice a dozen potatoes thin, also ¼ lb. fat salt pork, put into a pudding dish in alternate layers, seasoning with salt and pepper (only a little of the former). Bake, covered, ½ hour, uncover and brown.

Pork and Apples. Fruits seasoned with meat juices and fats, instead of with sugar, are not enough known among us.

Slice sour apples round in slices ⅓ in. thick without peeling, and fry with strips of pork or bacon. Serve together.

FRESH FISH.

The varieties of fresh fish are numberless, and to cook and serve them in perfection requires careful study from the cook. The subject must here be treated very briefly.

Fresh fish may be cooked in any of the ways applicable to meat; the length of time being much shorter, and care being required on account of the delicacy of the fibre. This makes broiling somewhat difficult.

Small fish are perhaps best egged and bread crumbed and fried in hot fat.

Fish Chowder. This dish deserves especial mention because of its cheapness and good flavor. It may be made of any fresh fish.

Fill a pudding dish with the fish cut in pieces, seasoning each layer with salt and pepper, and bits of suet or fat pork; put over it a potato crust as for meat pie (see page 46), or a soda biscuit crust, and bake. Bread crumbs or sliced potatoes may be mixed with the fish, and more seasoning used.

Fish Soups. Fresh fish can also be made into soups, and the cheaper kinds should be more used for this purpose.

Codfish Soup. Cook 1 tablespoon of flour in 1 tablespoon of butter. Add 1½ qts. milk, or milk and water, and when it boils stir in 1 teacup of cold boiled codfish that has been freed from skin and bones and then chopped fine or rubbed through a sieve. Add salt and pepper to taste.

Bullhead or Catfish Soup. An excellent soup can be made of this cheap fish.

Clean and cut up 2 or 3 lbs. and boil an hour in 2 qts. water with an onion and a piece of celery or any herbs (it must be well seasoned). Then add 1 cup of milk and a piece of butter or beef fat, or a piece of salt pork cut in bits may be boiled with the fish.

SALT FISH.

Salt Cod. This is one of the cheap foods that seems to be thoroughly appreciated among us, and good ways of cooking it are generally understood.

It must be freshened by laying it in water over night; put into cold water and bring gradually to a boil; set the kettle back where it will keep hot for half an hour, separate the flakes and serve with a milk sauce.

Fish Balls. This favorite dish is prepared by adding to codfish, boiled as above and finely shredded, a like quantity of mashed potato. Make into balls and fry on a griddle or in boiling fat.

Any other fish can be used in the same way.

FOWLS.

The flesh of fowls cannot rank among cheap foods, but in any economical family the Sunday dinner may often be a fricassee made of a fowl no longer young. Unless very ancient, the flavor of such a fowl will be richer than that of a chicken; we have but to cook it till it is tender.

Old Fowl Fricasseed. Cut into joints, put into cold water and bring slowly to a simmering heat; on no account let it boil,—keep it as nearly as possible at 170° for 3 or 4 hours, or till it is very tender. At the end of 2 hours, add a sliced onion and salt and thicken the gravy.

Chicken Soup. None but the wealthy should use chickens for soup, but from the bones left of baked or fricasseed chicken a good and economical soup can be made. Boil an hour or two, take out the bones, thicken a little and serve with bread dice fried in butter.

Giblet Soup. An excellent soup can be made of the *giblets*, that is, heart, liver and neck of chicken, and other fowls, which in city markets are sold separately and very cheap. Cut in small pieces and boil 2 hours with onion and herbs, then add a little butter and thickening, salt and pepper.

EGGS.

The importance of eggs is to be estimated from various points of view; their food value is great, their digestibility when fresh is almost perfect, and they can be cooked in so many ways and are a necessary ingredient of so many dishes, that the cook could ill spare them. Indeed, in all countries, their consumption seems to be limited only by their price.

Freshness. After the first twenty-four hours an egg steadily deteriorates. Physicians say, "never give to an invalid an egg that is more than two or three days old."

There are methods in use for preserving eggs fresh, on the principle of excluding air by sealing up the pores of the shell, but none of them are without risk and they cannot be recommended to one who must economize closely. It is better to go without eggs as nearly as possible in winter.

Raw Eggs. Eggs are as digestible raw as cooked, and one easily comes to like the taste of a fresh raw egg beaten to a foam and mixed with a little milk or water and sugar flavored with a little nutmeg or jelly.

Soft Boiled Eggs. To soft boil an egg its temperature should not be raised above 170°. The white will then be a jelly-like, digestible substance, but if exposed to a higher temperature, the white becomes horny while the yolk remains uncooked or becomes pasty. There are two methods of boiling an egg properly, which may be adopted according to convenience.

1st. Allow 1 qt. of boiling water to 4 eggs. Use a pail or jar (heated before the water is put in) and wrap around with a flannel cloth. The eggs will be done in 6 minutes, but are not harmed by ten.

2d. Put the eggs into cold water and bring slowly to a boil. They are done when the water begins to boil.

Hard Boiled Eggs. To boil an egg hard, it is no more necessary to expose it to a high degree of heat than in the case of the soft boiled; the heat must simply be much longer continued, 20 minutes to a half hour. The egg will then be solid but not horny as when cooked in boiling water.

A great many attractive dishes can be made of cold boiled eggs.

Scrambled, poached, omelet, and baked eggs. These are but different modes of cooking eggs soft or solid. The taste will be more delicate and they will be more digestible if in these cases also only the low degree of heat above mentioned be applied—more time being given them than is usually allowed.

EGG DISHES.

These dishes under many names and in many forms are of next importance after meats, composed, as they generally are, of eggs and vegetables or some preparation of the grains, while numberless additions and flavors are used to give variety and make the dish tempting to the eye and palate. Eggs so prepared have their full nutritive value; not so in rich puddings and cakes, where they are mixed with more sugar and fat than the system can take up in any quantity.

The following are a few recipes that have not been included under other heads. Many others will be found under the Cooking of the Grains.

Bread omelet. 1 cup of hard bread partly softened in hot water and milk, or in cold water (in which case press in a cloth and crumble), add ½ of a chopped onion, 1 tablespoon chopped parsley, 1 egg, salt and pepper. Heat in the frying pan or square baking pan, some bits of suet or beef fat, and pour in the omelet. Cover and bake five minutes, then uncover and brown. Or it may be cooked slowly on top of the stove. Cut in pieces and serve around the meat or with a gravy.

Egged bread. Bread, fresh or stale, is cut in long strips, or in squares or rounds with a cake cutter. Let them soak till soft but not broken, in 1 pt. of salted milk into which two eggs have been beaten. Bake a nice brown or fry on a griddle in half suet and half butter. (May be made with one egg.)

Potato omelet. Fry a small onion, sliced, in a teaspoonful of butter or fat; fill the pan with 2 cups of cold sliced potatoes, salt and pepper them, and pour over them 2 beaten eggs. Bake slowly till it is just solid and turn out carefully on a platter. *Or*, 1 cup potatoes and 1 cup bread crumbs may be used.

Rice omelet. 1 cup cold boiled rice, 2 teaspoons milk, 1 egg, ½ teaspoon salt. Mix and pour into a pan in which a tablespoon of butter has been heated. Fry and double over when done. *Or*, it may be baked like potato omelet.

Flour omelet. 1 egg, 1 cup milk, 2 tablespoons flour, pinch of salt, add the beaten white of the egg last.

This is the "Yorkshire Pudding" which is cooked in the pan over which beef is roasting; it is cut in squares and served around the meat. It may also be baked in a buttered pan without meat.

Tomato omelet. 3 eggs, 1 cup flour (scant), 1 tablespoon fine herbs, salt and cayenne pepper, 1 tablespoon sugar, juice of 2 large tomatoes and 1 cup warm milk. Bake under roasting meat, or alone in a buttered pan.

CHEESE DISHES.

Almost any cheese will give a good result in these dishes. Crumbly cream cheese is richer in taste and has also been shown to be more quickly digested. Skim cheeses are as nutritious except in fat, and in some dishes, as in "Fondamin" give a better result. Grate old cheeses, chop new and soft ones.

Grated cheese. Grate old cheese and serve with bread and butter. It is also a good addition to mashed potato, to flour porridges, to oatmeal and and wheat flour porridges, to rice, sago, tapioca and indeed to any starchy foods; it should be stirred in while these are quite hot. Its use with macaroni is given elsewhere.

Cooked cheese with bread. The basis of these dishes is toasted bread (white or graham) arranged on a platter, and enough salted water poured on to soften it.

1. Grate enough old cheese to cover the toast prepared as above. Set in the oven to melt, and put the slices together as sandwiches. This is the simplest form of "Welsh Rarebit.'

2. ½ lb. cheese, 1 tablespoon butter and 1 cup milk. Stir till smooth over a gentle fire or in a water bath and spread over the toast.

3. ¼ lb. cheese, 1 tablespoon butter, 2 egg yolks, ½ teaspoon mustard, a pinch of cayenne pepper. Stir to smooth paste, spread on the toast and set in a hot oven for 4 minutes.

4. To each person allow 1 egg, 1 tablespoon grated cheese, ½ teaspoon butter or 1 tablespoon milk, a little salt and pepper (cayenne best). Cook like custard in a pail set in a kettle of hot water, stirring till smooth, it may then be used on toast or poured out on a platter. It may also be steamed 5 minutes in little cups, or baked very slowly for 10 minutes.

5. Slices of bread lightly buttered, 3 eggs, 1½ cups milk, 1 teaspoon salt, 1 cup grated cheese. Soak the bread in the milk and egg till soft but not broken. Lay the pieces in a pan, cover with the cheese and bake or steam.

Fondamin or Fondue. This is a famous foreign dish, and although it may seem to have a good many ingredients, it is really not much trouble to make.

¼ lb. of grated cheese (skim better than cream) add to 1 gill of milk, in which is as much bicarbonate of potash as will lie on a three cent piece, ¼ teaspoon mustard, ½ saltspoon white pepper, a few grains of cayenne, 1 oz. butter, a grating of nutmeg and 2 tablespoons baked flour. Heat carefully till the cheese is dissolved. Add 3 beaten eggs and stir till smooth. This mixture should be baked separately for each person in patty pans or paper cases and eaten immediately. All cheese dishes should be served very hot.

MILK.

Milk is sometimes called the one perfect food, containing all the constituents in their right proportions. This is true only for the requirements of a baby, but it remains for any age a valuable food when rightly supplemented.

Milk contains on the average 3.31% proteids, 3.66% fat, 4.9% carbohydrates, 87.41% water, and .70% salts.

The housewife, if she wishes to use milk with economy, will not in cooking use it *as such*, but with due regard to the different values of the cream and the skim parts. In cities skim milk is sold for about one-half the price of full milk, and is well worth it if pure, but it is too often mixed with water.

Boiling Milk. As soon as milk comes into the house it should be boiled, as it is a notorious carrier of disease germs which only in this way can be killed. Use an earthenware pitcher and let the milk remain standing in the same after cooking. The next day remove the cream for the morning's coffee, and use the skim part during the day for cooking, with or without the addition of a little butter.

Keeping Milk. To keep milk sweet in warm weather is a serious question to the housekeeper who has no cellar or refrigerator. It is of first importance that the vessels used to contain it should be scrupulously clean. Boiling, as above mentioned, and cooling it rapidly afterwards, will keep it sweet for 24 hours, unless the weather is very warm, and the time may be further extended by keeping the milk pitcher set in a dish of cold water. A quarter of a teaspoonful of baking soda to a quart of milk, added while it is still sweet, may be used in case of necessity but this is not to be commended for common use.

Canning Milk. A method that the writer has employed is this: simply canning the milk as one would can fruit. Fill glass jars and screw down the lids, then place them in a steamer over cold water; heat the water gradually and steam the jars for an hour, then tighten the tops. I have never kept milk so treated for more than a week, but see no reason why it should not keep much longer.

Sour Milk. However, if you find yourself with sour milk on your hands, do not throw it away, it has many uses. Buttermilk is also very valuable to the housewife; it can be kept a long time in good condition for mixing doughs by covering with water, which must, however, be often changed for fresh.

USES FOR SOUR MILK AND BUTTERMILK.

Bonny Clabber. Put skim milk into a glass dish or into tea cups and set away until it becomes solid. Then eat with sugar and powdered cinnamon sprinkled over it.

Cottage Cheese. Set thick sour milk where it will heat gradually till the curd separates, then pour into a bag and let it drip till dry. Salt well, and add a little cream or milk and melted butter.

Buttermilk.

1st. As a drink. For this it should be very fresh.

2d. Buttermilk soup. (See page 123.)

Uses for both.

Both buttermilk and sour milk can be used

1st. In making soda biscuit dough (see page 102.)

2d. In pancakes of all kinds (see page 103.)

3d. In corn bread (see page 103.)

4th. In some kinds of cake, as in gingerbread, cookies and doughnuts, where they are by many cooks preferred to sweet milk; and in almost any kind of cake sour milk may be substituted for sweet, remembering always to use only half the quantity of cream of tartar called for in the recipe.

FATS AND OILS.

The third food principle, Fats, stands between the two great nutrients, Proteids on the one hand and Carbohydrates on the other, and we find that we can indulge in considerable latitude as to its use. When we wish to get our food in a more condensed form, we can use fats freely in connection with proteids and lessen the amount of carbohydrates. In army dietaries the amount of fat is largely increased for marching, and for great exertion the quantity becomes three times that allowed in garrison life. For instance, the daily rations served out to the German soldiers in France during the month of August, 1870, contained

	Proteids	Fats	Carbohydrates
Army Dietary.	157 gms.	285 gms.	331 gms.

It was represented by 1 lb. 10 oz. of bread, about 1⅛ lbs. of meat, and over ½ lb. of bacon besides an allowance of coffee, tobacco and wine or beer. Prof. Ranke has called this an admirable diet for fighting men. In garrison life these soldiers would have received only 56 grams of fat, and 120 grams of proteids while the carbohydrates would have been increased to 500 grams or more.

On the other hand, fat when coupled with enough carbohydrate food can replace some of the proteid, and often does so in the food of hardy and econom-

Diet of Bavarian Woodchopper.

ical people. The Bavarian woodchopper is enabled by his splendid digestion to arrange his diet in the following way: he takes little proteid from the animal kingdom, but in order to get enough of it from vegetable products, he must, as we know, take in an immense quantity of the starch associated with it, and to this he adds a great quantity of fat. Von Liebig says that such a man takes on the average

Proteids	Fats	Carbohydrates
112 gms.	309 gms.	691 gms.

We see therefore that we can have a sliding scale for fat; that while we should not go below 2 oz. a day, we may, in case we lower one or both of the other two great constituents, go up to 8 or 9 oz.

Importance of Fat not realized.

People belonging to the well-to-do classes, unless they have given special study to the subject, seldom realize the importance of fat in our economy. Fat means to them fat meat, suet, lard and the like, and the much eating of these is considered proof of a gross appetite; they do not consider how much fat they take in eggs, in milk, in grains like oatmeal and maize, in the seasoning of their varied dishes, and in their well-fattened meats, where, as in an average piece from a very fat mutton, they eat twice as much fat as proteid without knowing it.

Indeed, a well fed man of the upper classes may have more fat in his daily diet than has the freshly arrived Mechlenburg laborer who spreads a quarter inch layer of lard on his bread. The latter cannot take his fat in unsuspected forms; he craves this principle with his plain vegetable diet, and must take it as he can get it.

Now let us understand that where economy is to be considered, this question of fat does not take care of itself as it does for the rich man. The economical housewife should always keep in mind that she must furnish her family enough fat, and furnish it cheaply.

Substitutes for Butter. Butter is a dear fat; count out the water in it and see what it costs you. We must economize in butter in as many ways as possible. We must eat more fat meat, first, that which is ingrained with the lean where it takes the place of water, as we have seen under "Proteids," costing us practically nothing; when we eat our vegetables seasoned with such a piece of meat, we find them sufficiently seasoned. We must also eat more of fat meat which we recognize as such, taking pains to cook it so that it will be palatable; the crisp, brown outside of a roast is always welcome, but the fat of boiled beef or mutton will also be relished if served very hot. An excellent selection in low-priced beef, is the fat middle rib; the lean part is very tender and juicy when cooked in water at a low temperature for two or three hours (or in Heat Saver, see page 44, for three or four hours) and the fat, if served hot, any but a pampered taste will relish. Too much cannot be said in praise of pork as furnishing a good tasting and cheap fat; it can be cooked in many ways and used to flavor vegetables, etc.

Digestibility of Fat. It is consoling to the economist to know that little of this food principle will be wasted in the body. Fat is more completely absorbed, according to the testimony of the experimenters, than any other kind of food, even meat.

We want to say a few words as to the character of different animal fats, and then we are done with this subject.

All the fats consumed by us, without exception, are composed of three bodies called neutral fats, mixed together in varying proportions. These three bodies are "olein," "palmatin" (margarin), and "stearin," and the chief difference between them is that they melt at different temperatures; the more olein a fat has, the more easily it melts, and the less it has, the more it is like tallow. In vegetable oils, we find in addition to these, small quantities of what are called "fatty acids," and in butter we have beside the three common fats, a small per cent of four scarcer ones.

Fats compared.

Practically therefore, all fats are alike, and when absorbed they do the same work in the body, their varying flavors and their colors having nothing to do with this.

However, their flavor, their appearance and the ease with which they melt in the mouth and in the digestive tract have much to do with our estimation of them as foods. Mutton fat will do our body the same service as butter, but because of the relatively small amount of olein it contains, we have difficulty in swallowing it.

As to the comparative digestibility of these fats, it is generally admitted that those which melt at a low temperature, like butter and vegetable oils, are most readily taken up by the system; it is thought that we could digest beeswax if it would melt in the stomach. Still, although butter stands in common estimation as the most digestible, as it is the most palatable of the fats, the stomach finds no trouble in disposing of reasonable amounts of any fat used in the household.

Artificial Butter. The fact that all fats are so similar in composition, and that, if once digested, they will do the same service in the body, first led scientists to try to make out of the cheaper fats a substitute for butter. It was Napoleon III who set the chemist Mège-Mourier at work to discover an artificial butter for use in the army. This chemist added butter color and flavors made in the laboratory, to olein and margarin extracted from beef suet, and mixed with this a little real butter, and so successful was the result, that the making of artificial butter has become a great industry. Now certainly no one objects to artificial butter on the ground that it is made of animal fats, for he eats these every day on his table; he objects because he has doubts as to the cleanliness or the healthfulness of its method of manufacture.

Therefore since the substitution, to some extent, of animal fats for butter is from an economic standpoint so desirable, if we cannot bring ourselves to use oleomargarine we must do the best we can in these kitchen laboratories of ours to make other fats than butter acceptable to the taste.

USES OF FATS.

Beef Suet. Its Uses. Beef suet has many uses. It should be bought perfectly fresh, that surrounding the kidneys being chosen as of the best quality. Chopped fine, it is used in suet puddings, and may be employed to enrich other puddings made of skim milk, as a rice pudding; it combines well with bread crumbs in any hot dish, in bread puddings, bread stuffing, bread omelet and soup balls. In all cases it must be chopped fine and cooked sufficiently to fully incorporate it with the other materials. Suet may also be used in many flour dishes instead of butter, if they are only cooked long enough and eaten warm, also in all cake where molasses and spices or any strong flavor is used.

Marrow. Every bit of marrow in bones should be scraped out and carefully used. Its taste is more delicate than that of suet, and it can be substituted for butter even in fine cake.

Butter tried out. Whatever butter you use in cooking should be *cooked* butter which may be prepared when butter is cheap and put away for winter use. So prepared it will keep as long as lard. A second quality of butter may be used for this, or that which is beginning to be rancid; if already so, add ¼ teaspoon soda to each pound, but such butter when tried out will not keep as long as that made from sweet butter. In trying out butter great care must be taken not to burn it. Put it in a large iron kettle and cook it down very slowly until you no longer hear the sound of boiling; it will then begin to froth and rise and this is a sure sign that the process is completed. Set the kettle back to cool a few moments, then skim and pour off the butter from the dregs into jars. Keep in a cool place and closely covered. In any recipe use ¼ less than of fresh butter.

Tried out Suet. This should be done with even more care, to avoid the tallowy flavor. Exact directions are given in "Cooking Methods," page 41. The "scraps" are often relished by children.

This beef fat (which we decline to call tallow) should be put away in cakes in a jar closely covered.

To use. To use it, scrape it fine, sprinkling a little flour in it to keep it light. So prepared it may be used in any of the ways mentioned under "suet," and to this list still others may be added, since it does not need, as does suet, long cooking in order to mix it well with the other ingredients of the dish. It can be used successfully in warm breads of all kinds, and in all but the nicest cakes if mixed with ½ butter.

Lard. Much of the lard now furnished is so poor, that unless one pays a high price to a well known dealer, it is better for each housekeeper to buy the leaf lard and try it out herself.

Cut fine and cook all the water out, taking care not to burn.

The "scraps" are even better than those left from suet and should by no means be thrown away.

SAUCES FOR MEAT AND VEGETABLES.

The economical and busy housewife says she has no time nor money for sauces, but the fact is she cannot afford to do without them.

All vegetables must have some fat to season them and to use butter in every case is extravagant and gives no variety, while a cheaper fat if made into a sauce with flour and water, can be flavored in a dozen ways.

DRAWN BUTTER SAUCES.

Drawn butter, which is the foundation of most of the sauces is thus made.

Plain. A heaping tablespoon of butter or beef fat is put into a saucepan; when it boils, 1 heaping tablespoon flour is added and stirred as it cooks. To this add gradually 1 pt. of water, 1 teaspoon salt and ¼ teaspoon of pepper. If you wish to unite economy and good flavor use ½ tablespoon of beef fat in making the sauce, and add ½ tablespoon butter, cut in little pieces, just before serving.

Milk sauce is the same, made with milk instead of water.

In *brown sauce*, the fat and flour are stirred till they brown, then make as above.

Any number of sauces can be made from these three by adding different flavors; chopped pickles and a tablespoon vinegar are added to No. 1 when it is to be used on fish; or mustard for mustard sauce.

The addition of eggs raw or cooked makes another variety.

Milk gravies. With the help of milk we can make a gravy as in "milk sauce," with beef or pork fat, seasoning with salt and pepper and perhaps some powdered herb.

Children like all these gravies, if nicely made and flavored, to eat on bread as well as on vegetables.

MEAT SAUCES.

A few cheap sauces for meats alone deserve special mention.

Mint sauce. 2 tablespoons green mint or spear mint chopped, 1 tablespoon sugar, ½ cup vinegar. Mix and let stand an hour or two.

Tomato sauce. Boil 1 pt. fresh or canned tomatoes with a little onion, salt, and herb flavoring until quite thick, then strain and add 1 teaspoonful of flour cooked in a teaspoonful of butter.

Fruit sauce. Any sour fruit, as apples or plums, makes an excellent sauce to eat with meat. Apple sauce goes especially well with pork.

Horseradish sauce. Add to drawn butter or any meat gravy ½ cup grated horseradish. Simmer a few minutes.

CARBOHYDRATE-CONTAINING FOODS

AND THEIR PREPARATION.

We are now to furnish for the body the third great food principle, the carbohydrates. These we mean when we speak of the starches and sugars, and with unimportant exceptions, they are furnished by the vegetable world only.

Cellulose. As we have seen, that troublesome body, cellulose, plays here a large rôle. It is the skeleton, so to speak, of plants, built by them out of sugar and starch; the chemist finds no difficulty in his laboratory in turning it back into dextrin and sugar, and our stomachs too can digest a large part of the cellulose of very young and tender plants,—from 47% to 62% it has been found, of young lettuce, celery, cabbage and carrots,—but in older plants, the cellulose proper becomes all intergrown and encrusted with substances of a woody and mineral nature, from which even the chemist separates it with the greatest difficulty, while our digestive juices are entirely unequal to the task. Therefore it is that the whole art of the cook is needed in treating this substance; she must soften it, she must break it up, and in many cases separate it as completely as possible from the sugars, starches and proteids which it hinders us from appropriating to our use.

Its use. In some cases, as in oatmeal and graham flour, we leave the cellulose because of its mechanical action on the bowels. To be sure, this is a wasteful process, for the cellulose carries with it when it leaves the body considerable undigested food, but better this waste than to give the muscles of our intestines so little work to do that they become unable to digest any but fine, condensed foods.

As a rule, however, we must think of cellulose not as a food at all, but as a tough, foreign body which we must reckon with before we can utilize the proteid and starch particles of many important vegetable foods.

Amount of Carbohydrate. The carbohydrates, especially the starches, are the cheapest of the food constituents and therefore most apt to be in excess, especially in the food of the poor. According to estimates already given, an adult at average hard work gets along nicely with 1⅛ lbs. of carbohydrate material (meaning, of course, the dry amount of this one principle), though fortunately, as mentioned under "Fats," it is found that some of this large amount can be exchanged for fat, if the body, for any reason can better use the latter. Brainworkers and the richer classes the world over take less of carbohydrates, at least in their starch form, and more proteids and fats.

Inasmuch as we get these carbohydrates from the vegetable kingdom, and because the housewife must furnish them combined with other principles as in bread and other things made of flour, and in various dishes in which vegetables are combined with meat, milk, eggs, etc., we will cease speaking of carbohydrates as such, and will give a few hints as to how to prepare vegetable foods so that we can get the most out of them, bearing in mind, however, what has been said about not following out this principle to the extent of weakening the bowels.

To what extent digested.

This leads us, first, to examine the general digestibility of the whole class of vegetable foods; meaning by this, not the rapidity nor the ease, but the *extent* to which the nutritive principle is yielded up to us. It has been found that, as usually prepared, vegetable foods give up to us from ¼ to ½ less of their nutrients than do animal foods, and especially is this true of those that are rich in proteids. To illustrate: a workman eats as part of his dinner a dish of boiled beans, but though he rightly considers that he has been eating a nourishing dish, he has really absorbed only 60% of the nitrogenous substances contained in it, the other 40% passing from him unused because of its intimate connection with the cellulose; at least this was the case with Prof. Strümpell who records the result of personal experiments on the digestibility of beans cooked whole. Now this workman digested of the meat part of his dinner 97½%, and this comparison shows how the tougher kinds of cellulose interfere with the absorption of the food matters which they enclose.

The starch part of vegetable food we seem to get out much better than the proteid part, even with our ordinary methods of cooking; thus out of cooked rice we get almost 99% of the starch, but only 80% of what proteid it contains; flour in the form of noodles and macaroni yields up 98½% of its starch and 80% of its albumen,—in the form of bread a little less of each. The potato will give us only 75% of what little proteid it contains, but as high as 92.5% of its starch.

Effect of too much starch in the diet.

Although the starch-containing foods are cheap and although they yield up a good per cent of this nutritive principle, they must not be used to excess for the following reason. Starch must first be turned into sugar by our digestive juices before it can be taken up into the blood, and if the stomach is given more at a time than it can master, certain fermentations may take place, and digestion be influenced. The best authorities say that without doubt the continued and severe diarrheas of small children are due to the fermentation of starch foods for which their digestive organs are not yet ready.

These fermentations, the irritating action on the bowels of too much cellulose, and the loss of a good deal of proteid substance connected with it form the shady side of a vegetable diet. Even the ox with his many stomachs gets out of grass and unchopped hay only 60% of the proteid and 50% of the fat contained in it.

VEGETABLE PROTEIDS.

Even in our part of the world two thirds of the proteid food of most people is taken from the vegetable kingdom, and in order to choose our food profitably, we must know where to look for vegetable proteids, and how to fit them for eating. Here the cereals and the legumes are our friends, the former furnishing from 7 to 14% in their dried state, the latter giving the astonishing figure of 20 to 24%; or as much as meat.

GRAINS.

The cereals or grains, though containing much less proteid than the legumes, are more valuable to us because of their excellent taste, their availability to the cook and the readiness with which when ground they yield us their nutrients.

Since the grains are such important foods, a table is appended showing the average richness in food principles of those in common use among us. We find that different analyses of the same grain differ greatly from one other, barley for instance, ranging from 8 to 18% in its proteid, and this may account for a certain grain being popular in one country and not in another.

In our country we are especially fortunate in the cheapness and excellence of at least two of the grains, Wheat and Indian Corn. The first has of course much higher food value, but the latter is so cheap and can be so easily cooked that it is a blessing to the poor. The large per cent of both proteids and fat in oats is to be noted, justifying as it does, the high esteem in which they are now held among us. At the other extreme is rice, the poorest of the grains in both these principles, but its almost perfect digestibility renders it very useful.

Wheat and Indian Corn.

Oats.

Rice.

Analysis of Grains.	Proteids %	Fats %	Carbo-hydrates %	Water %	Cellulose %
Fine Wheat Flour	10.	1.0	75.2	13.	0.3
Rye Flour......	11.5	2.	69.5	14.	1.5
Barley Grits.....	11.	1.5	71.5	15.	0.5
Oat Grits.......	14.5	6.0	65.	10.	2.5
Buckwheat Flour	9.5	2.	72.5	14.	1.
Corn or Maize Flour	10.15	4.80	68.45	14.	2.6
Rice Grains.....	8.	1.	76.5	13.	0.5

SUGARS.

Most people would class sugar among the luxuries, and indeed we are best acquainted with it in those combinations with fruit, eggs, butter, and various flavoring matters, which, as puddings, pies, cakes, custards, etc., make up our dessert list.

Food Value. Our first concern, however, is with its food value. It gives us the high figure of 99% of the third food principle,—Carbohydrates. That is, it must be put in the list with bread and it can be used to a certain extent instead of bread and other starch foods. Moreover, it is especially fitted for a food in cases where nourishment is needed immediately, as it is digested or absorbed into the system almost as quickly as water and without taxing the digestive organs, and perhaps on this account is its consumption so great in our country; we live fast, and we want our nutriment in a condensed form.

But on account of its cost and because we are able

to take only a moderate amount at a time, sugar cannot, to any great extent, take the place of the starches; we are to value it chiefly for the relish it gives to other foods. As a flavor, it is of the greatest value, but if we prize variety we are certainly accustomed to the taste of sugar in too many dishes, as in rice, custards, and various egg and bread dishes, which the foreigner would sometimes salt instead of sweeten, and eat with his meat instead of at the end of the meal.

Its chief value.

We would suggest that when we do use sugar, as in a pudding, for instance, that we use less of it than we are accustomed to do, for in that case we could eat enough of a dish so flavored to make it furnish more of the real substance of a meal.

BEANS, PEAS AND LENTILS.

Per cent of Proteids.

Look again at the remarkable per cent of proteid given by this class of vegetables. Beans and peas, 23%, Lentils, 25%, while beef gives on the average only from 17 to 21%. By people who from choice or necessity live principally on vegetables, the legumes have always been largely used; their consumption is extensive in India, China, and in all of Europe.

To be sure, the *quality* of the proteid is not the same as in meat,—it is less stimulating and palatable, and perhaps in other ways inferior, but the proteid needs of the body can be answered by it, and that is a very important item when the question is one of economy.

Digestibility.

The impression that dried beans and peas are "hearty" food, fitted for outdoor workers rather than for less vigorous people or those of sedentary habits, seems justified by the fact that these vegetables contain an unusually large per cent of cellulose of the tougher sort which requires a long continued application of heat to free it from the proteid and starch of the vegetable; indeed, unless it is broken fine or ground into flour, cooking, however long continued, will be insufficient. We have seen that Prof. Strümpell digested only 40% of the proteid of beans cooked in the ordinary way, but when they were ground to flour and baked he digested 91.8% The fact is, we could cook and eat our wheat whole much more easily than we can our beans, and yet bean flour is not in the market, if we except the "prepared" sort in small, expensive packages. It seems that the best we can do is to cook beans well and sieve them; in that way we free them from the skins at least.

Cellulose.

Bean Flour.

Split Pea.

The dried and split pea, though as valuable as the bean and already freed from the skin, is not as much used among us; it should be more employed in soups and as a vegetable.

Lentils a few years ago were to be found only in large cities; now they are more easily attainable. Their food value, as we have seen, is still greater than that of beans and peas, but the taste is not as agreeable until one becomes accustomed to it. An economist cannot afford to neglect the legume family.

POTATÓES.

We in our country need not feel as bitter against

the potato as do the scientists of Europe, for we are not obliged to use it to excess, and considering its cheapness and availability it is for us a good vegetable and on these accounts, though it makes a poor enough showing as to food value, we must rank it next to the bean in importance. It has only 2% of proteids, no fat and only 20.7% carbohydrates, and yet since it can be prepared in so many ways and we never tire of its mild flavor, it will doubtless continue to come upon our tables more frequently than any other vegetable. But every day or twice a day, in large amounts, is far too often; indeed those who use it to this extent must be ignorant of its relatively low food value. The quality of the potato is of great importance and none but the best should be used. It should be a mealy variety and perfectly ripe.

GARDEN VEGETABLES.

Green vegetables, excepting the pea and bean, are not to be valued chiefly for what we can reckon up in them of proteids, fats and carbohydrates, for the amount is very small. Except in the height of the season they must be looked on as luxuries, but we will buy them as often as we can afford them. In quantities sufficient to flavor soups and stews they can always be afforded, and in this way should be freely used, carrots, celery, parsnips, and tomatoes, for example.

FRUITS.

Our markets offer us a great variety of fine fruits, and many of them are cheap in their season; apples in the fall are within the reach of the very poorest.

Fresh fruits have a large per cent of water, as high as 89% in the orange, and few fruits have less than 80%. Their food value is mainly in the form of sugar, apples giving us on an average 7.7%, grapes, 14.3%; of proteids, the amount does not, with the single exception of the strawberry, reach 1%; but fruits are very useful to us on account of their flavor, due to various aromatic bodies, fruit acids and sugar. The apple is especially valuable on account of its cheapness and fine keeping qualities, and is used in a variety of ways by the cook to give a relish to plain materials. Although our largest use of them is in sweet dishes, they are perhaps quite as valuable used without sugar; they may be fried in slices and eaten with fat meat, as bacon or sausage, or they may be used to stuff a fowl.

Fruit is not for all people easy of digestion if eaten in considerable quantities, and this is partly on account of its relatively large per cent of woody fibre, and also, especially when not quite ripe, because of the acids and pectose contained in them. Huckleberries have 12% woody fibre, apples only 2% including the seeds and skin.

The importance of dried fruits as food is not well enough understood. Fruit loses in drying a large portion of its water, leaving its nutritive parts in more condensed form for our use; dried apples are very near to bread in the per cent of nutrients they offer, and the dried pear may be called the date of Germany, so general is its use. With us this fruit is too expensive, but in parts of Germany the writer has seen dried pears commonly exposed for sale by the barrel like beans; they are eaten in great quantities by the common people, who seem to digest them and dried apples without any trouble, accustomed as their stomachs are to a rye bread and vegetable diet. These dried fruits are made into a variety of dishes with meats, with potatoes and with beans and also with noodles and macaroni.

COOKING OF GRAINS.

The grains may be cooked whole, coarsely ground, as grits, and finely ground, as flour.

Grains cooked whole. All these grains can be cooked whole but it is seldom done, because of the length of time required. Only rice and barley are generally so cooked.

Rice. To cook. In cooking rice, the aim should be to have the grains distinct from each other, soft, dry and mealy.

Steamed. This is the best way. Add to the rice three times its bulk of water, salt well, put in a covered dish in a steamer and steam ½ hour. Or, the rice may be soaked over night, and it will then steam soft in twenty minutes.

Boiled. Put the rice into a large quantity of boiling water, add one teaspoon salt to each cupful of rice; boil fast, stirring occasionally. Drain, dry out a little and keep warm by covering with a cloth, as is done with potatoes. Save the water poured off for soup.

Rice. To use. Its best use is as a vegetable with meat. Being of a bland and neutral character, it can, like bread, be made into an endless number of dishes to be eaten with meats, or into dessert dishes, with sugar, fruits, etc. For rice omelette (see page 60), rice pudding (see pages 107 and 110).

Grated cheese is a good addition to rice, supplying its lack of proteids and fat.

Pearl barley boiled. Soak all night and boil soft in salted water. It may also be steamed. Use as a thickening for soups, or like rice, as a vegetable, or as a breakfast dish with sugar and milk.

With prunes. It is excellent mixed with its bulk of stewed prunes;—pour over it melted butter, sugar and cinnamon.

GRAINS, COARSELY GROUND, OR GRITS.

These are better adapted to simple cookery than are fine flours, since to make them eatable it is only necessary to cook them soft in water. The grains used in this way among us are cracked wheat, farina or wheat grits, oatmeal, hominy and corn meal, and they are all cooked in nearly the same way.

MUSHES.

Wheat, oat and corn mushes. *Time* 2–3 hours. This time may be shortened by soaking the grits some hours in water. Oatmeal and corn cannot be overcooked.

Amount of Water. They all, except corn, absorb from three to four times their bulk of water; corn, a little over twice.

Salt. One teaspoonful to one cupful of grits.

Method of cooking. Steaming is best, as there is then no danger of burning or of making the mush pasty by stirring. Put the grits and four times their bulk of water into a double boiler or into a dish and set the dish into a steamer, or use a tin pail with tight cover, and set in a kettle of water;—any way to keep it at boiling heat without burning.

Uses for cold mushes.

Porridge. Stir any cold cooked mush smooth with half water and half milk to the consistency of porridge. Add a little salt and boil up. Sugar and cinnamon or nutmeg may be added as flavor. Of course porridges can be also made of the uncooked grits, they are simply very thin mushes.

Pancakes. 1 cup of cold oatmeal, hominy or corn mush, 2 cups flour, ½ pint of milk, ½ teaspoon salt, and 1 egg, 2 teaspoons baking powder or 1 of soda and 2 of cream of tartar. Or, sour milk may be used with 1 teaspoon soda, omitting the cream of tartar. These mushes will differ a little in thickness, and therefore more or less flour may be needed. Bake on griddle.

Muffins. The same mixture as above, with the addition of a little more flour. Bake in muffin rings.

To Fry. For this, only corn mush and hominy are commonly used. When cooking, add a handful of wheat flour to the mush to make it stiffer. Pack while warm into a square mould and when cold cut in slices and fry slowly to a nice brown on a griddle with a little fat. Or, the slices may be dipped into beaten egg, then into bread crumbs, and fried in boiling fat.

CORN FLOUR.

There is one fine flour that can be treated in the same way as the coarsely ground,—that made from

Indian corn. Perhaps on account of its larger per cent of fat and because little of its albumen is in the form of gluten, it does not form into a sticky paste as does wheat flour, but can be mixed with water only and then boiled or baked into digestible and good tasting food, and this is one thing that makes corn so valuable a grain to people like the negroes of the southern states, whose cooking apparatus is of the most primitive sort. Corn meal has one peculiarity,—it quickly sours and should be kept no longer than a week. The kiln-dried meal, however, keeps indefinitely, and is now largely used, but is not as sweet as the freshly ground. The name "meal" seems to be used for both the fine and coarsely ground.

Corn mush. This, whether made from fine or coarsely ground corn, is cooked like grits. See page 86.

Hoe cake or corn pone. 1 quart Indian meal, 1 teaspoon salt. Moisten to a dough with boiling water or milk; let it stand a few hours till it shows air bubbles on the surface, then make into thick cakes and bake in the oven, or cut in slices and fry in pork fat on a griddle. Break, not cut, and eat hot.

GRAHAM FLOUR.

This preparation of wheat, though finely ground, may be treated somewhat like grits, and a bread may be made of it with the addition of water only which will be light and palatable. The secret of success is in having the oven very hot.

Graham gems. Mix salted graham flour with cold water to a batter thick enough to drop, then put it into iron forms already heated, and bake in a *very* hot oven for about fifteen minutes.

FINE WHEAT FLOUR.

Flour may be cooked, of course, in boiling water or milk, and in this way is used to thicken gravies or soups, and also to make a sort of mush with milk and eggs. See "Minute Pudding," page 107.

The principle of cooking it in this case differs not at all from the cooking of a potato; in both cases the starch granules soak up the hot water till they burst their cellulose walls. But if we were to try to *bake* flour when wet up into a thick paste, we would find it, in the first place, difficult to accomplish, the heat being very slowly communicated from the surface to the interior, and when done, we would have only a tough indigestible mass. There is, however, one way of preparing such a paste for cooking, which we will consider before treating the "raising" of flour for bread. Flour dough is in this case kneaded hard, rolled thin and then dried. So treated we know it in the form of

MACARONI AND NOODLES.

Macaroni. A trade article extensively used abroad where the best kinds cost only ten to twelve cents a pound, and the broken or imperfect sticks not more than seven. It is a valuable article of food, but its use will not become extensive among us while it is so dear.

Like the fine flour of which it is principally composed it is deficient in fat, and must be eaten with the addition of butter, cheese or milk.

How cooked. Put into plenty of salted boiling water, and boil twenty or thirty minutes, till it is perfectly tender (if old it takes longer to cook).

8

Drain carefully, pouring it into a cullender or lifting out with a skimmer.

To Use. 1st. (Best.) Put it in the dish in layers with grated cheese and butter.

2d. Serve with milk and butter sauce.

3d. Add two beaten eggs to the milk and butter sauce.

Other Uses. Like bread and rice, macaroni when cooked is made into a great number of dishes; it is added to soups, it is mixed with meat in ragouts, and it is cooked with certain vegetables, as tomatoes.

With Tomatoes. Arrange the macaroni in a pudding dish in layers with grated cheese and stewed tomatoes. Brown in the oven.

Noodles. This is also a trade article, but that of home manufacture is much better. It may be called one of the German national dishes, so extensive is its use among that people, with whom it often constitutes the main dish of a meal without meat.

Ingredients. 3 eggs, 3 tablespoons milk or water, 1 teaspoon salt, and flour.

To make. Make a hole in the middle of the flour, put in the other ingredients and work to a stiff dough, then cut in 4 strips, knead each till fine grained, roll out as thin as possible and lay the sheet out to dry. When all are rolled begin with the first, cut it into 4 equal pieces, lay the pieces together and shave off very fine as you would cabbage, pick the shavings apart with floured hands and let them dry a little.

To use. Boil them a few at a time in salted water

taking them out with a skimmer and keeping them warm. Strew over them bread crumbs fried in butter or use like macaroni. (See page 90.)

These noodles will keep indefinitely when dried hard, therefore when eggs are cheap they may be made and laid up for the winter. The water in which they are boiled is the basis of Noodle Soup; it needs only the addition of a little butter, a tablespoonful of chopped parsley and a few of the cooked noodles.

Experimenters have proved that flour in the form of noodles and macaroni is more perfectly digested than even in bread.

BREAD MAKING.

Principles Involved. So far we have used in the cooking of flour no other principle than the simple application of water and heat. We must now consider how fine flour is to be made into what is known as bread. As before said, the particles easily pack together when wet into a pasty dough which, if so baked, would defy mastication and digestion. We must contrive in some way to separate these flour particles by forcing between them air or some other gas, so as to present as large a surface as possible to the action of the digestive juices and this may be done 1st, By surrounding these particles by fat, as in making pie-crust; 2d, By the air contained in beaten egg; 3d, By forcing carbonic acid gas through the mass by the action of (*a*) yeast, or (*b*) of bi-carbonate of soda acting on some acid.

FLOUR RAISED WITH FAT.

Pie-crust. The familiar example of this method is pie-crust, where a paste of water and flour is repeatedly rolled and spread with some fat, as lard, until the paste is in paper-thick layers with the fat between. When baked, the air expands and separates the flour particles, a true lightness being the result.

So much fat must be employed to produce this result, however, that the use of this method will of course be limited to the construction of dessert dishes, of which not much is eaten at once.

A flour rich in starch is better for this purpose than a gluten flour.

FLOUR RAISED WITH EGG.

The next most simple method of cooking fine flour, is to introduce between its particles the air adherent to beaten egg, and by the immediate application of heat to expand the air and stiffen the mass thus aerated. By this method none of the food principle is wasted as when yeast is used, nor is a chemical salt left in the dough as in the action of soda, but the method is expensive and is limited in its use to what may be called fancy breads and cakes.

We have selected the following mixture as the foundation for egg breads; of course others are possible:

Foundation of egg breads. 1 quart milk, 3 eggs, 1 tablespoon butter and 1 teaspoon salt.

This mixture is then thickened with any kind of flour, *or* with part flour and part bread, boiled rice, boiled hominy or corn mush.

To mix. First beat the eggs very light, whites and yolks separately, then the yolks smoothly with the flour and milk, stir the whites in at last very lightly and bake immediately. The eggs must be beaten *very* light, and the batter just of good pouring consistency, thinner than if no eggs were used.

Wheat, Graham or Corn Pancakes. Add to above foundation mixture a scant pint of either of these flours.

Cooked Rice, Hominy or Corn Mush Pancakes. Add to the foundation mixture one cup of flour and two cups of boiled rice, hominy or corn mush (or the proportions may be reversed). Bake in small, rather thick cakes. If they stick to the griddle add a little more flour.

Bread Pancakes. Add to the foundation mixture 1 cup flour and 2 cups bread crumbs that have been soaked soft in milk or water and mashed smooth. The batter should be rather thick. Bake in small cakes adding more flour if they stick.

Muffins and Waffles. Muffins and waffles of all sorts are made like pancakes, but a little stiffer with flour.

Other egg doughs. Other egg-raised doughs, mixed in somewhat different proportions and differently cooked, as fritters, sponge cakes and batter puddings, will be found in another section.

FLOUR RAISED WITH CARBONIC ACID GAS.

This is brought about by (*a*) the growth of the yeast plant or by the action (*b*) of bicarbonate of soda on some acid. Both of these methods have their advantages.

Yeast. The action of the yeast plant when brought into contact with flour and water is to develop carbon dioxide gas and alcohol. This it does at the expense of the little sugar already in the flour, but still more at the expense of that which it manufactures out of the starch, or as some say, out of the gluten. The chemist ascertains this loss of nutritive matter to be as high as 1%, and Liebig, who was strongly opposed to this method of bread raising, estimated that 40,000 people might be fed on the flour that was wasted in this way in Germany alone. But notwithstanding this waste, the method, on account of its convenience and the good taste it gives to bread, still holds its ground.

The time cannot be far distant when the baker will furnish us better and cheaper bread than we can make in our own kitchens. This has long been the case on the continent of Europe, but for some reason we have not yet reached that point in civilization and the housekeeper must still learn this art and practice it, for good bread is a necessity.

Quality of flour. The best flour is, even for the poor, the cheapest, as it makes more and better bread to the pound. There should always be two kinds kept on hand; the yellowish, high-priced gluten flour for bread making, and the whiter, cheaper sort for pastry, cake and thickenings.

No recipe for making yeast will be given, as the compressed yeast is so much better than the house-wife can make, and is now obtainable even in small towns.

To make bread. Proportions. 1 quart warm water, 2½ qts. (about) of flour, 1 tablespoon salt, 1 tablespoon or one cake of compressed yeast, or ½ cup liquid yeast. The proportions of flour and water differ according to the quality of the flour, the gluten flours taking up much more water than the starch flours.

Put the flour and salt into your bread pan and make a hole in the middle, then pour in gradually the water in which the yeast has been dissolved, mixing as you pour with your hand or with a spoon. As soon as the mass will hold together, take it out on a moulding board and with floured hands work it gradually into a tender dough, using as little flour as possible, for the dough must remain as soft as can be handled. This first moulding should take from 15 to 20 minutes. Then let the bread rise in a warm place; the yeast plant can live in a temperature ranging from 30° to 170° F. but thrives best at about 72°. Cover with a cloth and in winter keep by a warm stove. If made with compressed yeast, the dough will rise the first time in an hour. Take it at its first lightness, before it begins to sink back (it should be like a honeycomb all through, and double or treble its original bulk), put it on your moulding board, or ½ of it at a time, and mould it well until it is fine and tender again. Add no flour this time but keep the hands moist with warm water or milk or with lard. Divide into loaves—small ones—which should only half fill the greased tins, and set again to rise, keeping it at the same temperature and letting it get very light again. Flour that is rich in gluten requires longer to rise than that containing more starch.

Baking bread. It is difficult to give directions about the heat of the oven. One housekeeper says "hot enough so that you can hold your hand in till you count twelve," another, "until you can count thirty," and the puzzled novice can only inquire "how fast do you count?" The oven must be hot enough to brown the bread lightly in ten minutes, and to bake a small loaf in from twenty minutes to half an hour.

Additional facts. If more convenient, a bread sponge may be made at first with the water, yeast, and part of the flour, and when light, the rest of the flour added. It hastens the process a little.

How many times shall bread rise? Do not let the bread rise more than twice; it loses each time some of its nutritive qualities. Bread raised *once* is coarse of grain but sweet to the taste.

To keep bread long. Mould it harder than you do bread that is to be eaten soon.

Dough that has become chilled. Set the bread pan immediately into a larger one filled with warm water and as the water cools replace with warm until the dough begins to rise again.

Dough raised during the night. This method is often convenient, and does very well if slower yeast is used, but bread is better to be raised quickly with compressed yeast. If the latter is used a forenoon is sufficient for the process of making and baking.

To delay the baking of bread dough. For convenience, as to make warm biscuits for supper, rising dough may be kept at a standstill for hours without injury at a temperature of about 50°, as in a cellar, and an hour before baking brought into a warm room to finish the rising process.

BREADS FROM OTHER FLOURS.

Graham bread. Graham bread is made like white bread using two parts graham to one of white flour, or any other proportion liked, but it should be mixed very soft. A little sugar and fat should be added, 1 tablespoon lard or beef fat and 2 tablespoons sugar or molasses. Bake slower and longer than white bread.

The usual and most convenient way of making graham bread is to mix the flour and other ingredients with some of the white sponge on baking day.

Rye bread. Rye bread is made exactly as is bread from wheat flour, but in this country 4 parts rye, 1 part corn meal, and a handful of wheat flour are generally used. It must bake much longer —two to three hours in a slow oven. It is still better steamed the first two hours and baked the third.

Corn bread. Corn bread is made of 3 parts corn meal to 1 of wheat flour, same quantity of yeast and salt as for white bread, and an addition of 2 tablespoons lard or beef fat and two tablespoons sugar. It is only to be stirred, not moulded, and need rise but once.

BISCUITS, BUNS, ETC.

Breakfast rolls or biscuits. These are "little breads" of either white or graham flour. Make part of the dough out into little balls which will rise more quickly and bake in a shorter time, a little butter or lard, one tablespoon to a quart of dough being generally moulded with it.

When called "Breakfast Rolls" the dough is made out into flat round cakes, the top buttered and folded over not quite in the middle.

Milk rolls. Milk rolls are made from bread dough mixed with milk instead of water; they are very tender and delicate.

9

Wheat gems or drop biscuits. One modification in the baking of dough is worthy of mention. Use about a cup more milk in mixing the receipt for bread given above, so that the dough will just drop from a spoon and then bake in forms in the oven, or on a slow griddle.

Rusks. These are made from bread dough mixed with milk and with the addition of 4 eggs and 1 cup of butter to a quart of milk. Form, long and high.

Other uses for rusk dough. There are many uses for the above dough. When made out into biscuit shape it may be steamed and eaten as a simple pudding with fruit, or, made into tiny balls and cooked, when light, in a meat stew, the dish being then called a pot-pie.

Buns, plain. These are like *Rusks* (above) plus 2 cups of sugar and a little spice, say, ½ teaspoon nutmeg. Roll the dough out ½ inch thick, and cut with a biscuit cutter. Let it rise till very light, which will take some time on account of the sugar.

Fruit buns. To plain buns add 1 cup India currants, washed, dried and floured, or raisins cut in bits.

Raised Cake. From the recipe for Buns, as above, a plain and good cake may be made by using 1 pint instead of 1 quart of milk to the given quantity of eggs, butter and sugar, and adding a little more fruit. Bake in a ribbed pudding dish which has been thickly buttered, and in the butter, blanched almonds arranged in rows.

Doughnuts. Bun dough may also be fried in fat, as doughnuts.

For a fine brown crust. To give a fine crust to biscuit or buns: Brush over before baking, with a feather dipped in one of these mixtures: one teaspoon of molasses and milk, two teaspoons of sugar and milk, or three teaspoons sugar and the white of an egg.

To show the true relation of the above doughs to each other, the quantity has been kept the same as for bread dough, but one-half the given quantity of cake, buns or biscuit would be enough for a large family.

To steam bread. Any of the above doughs can be cooked by steaming instead of baking, when more convenient. They will of course lack the brown crust, but may afterward be dried or browned in the oven. A somewhat longer time is required for steaming than for baking.

YEAST BREADS — THIN.

Raised Pancakes. Wheat, Graham and Corn. The materials for these are, 1 qt. milk, or milk and water, a little more than a qt. of flour, 1 tablespoon compressed yeast or ½ cup liquid yeast, 1 teaspoon salt, 1 tablespoon butter; the flour may be wheat flour, wheat and graham mixed, or wheat and corn mixed, or part bread crumbs may be mixed with the flour. Make and raise like bread sponge. It is better they should be too thick than too thin, as milk may be added to thin them after they are light, but raw flour added at that time spoils them.

Pancakes with eggs. Add to the above batter just before baking, 1, 2 or 3 eggs, yolks and whites beaten separately. Use in this case somewhat less flour.

Muffins and Waffles. These can be made of either of the above pancake batters, with 1 cup to 1 pt. more flour.

BUCKWHEAT FLOUR.

Buckwheat flour makes bread that is relished by those accustomed to its somewhat peculiar taste, but in this country it is used only in pancakes.

Buckwheat Pancakes. 1 qt. buckwheat flour, 1 teaspoon salt, 1 cup or less of corn meal scalded in a little water, 2 teaspoons molasses (to make them brown—a little buttermilk answers the same purpose), 1 tablespoon compressed yeast, 1 qt. warm water, or enough to make a thin batter. Let rise over night.

FLOUR RAISED WITH SODA.

Soda. On the interaction of bicarbonate of soda and different acids, by which carbonic acid gas is liberated is based a common method of raising doughs. It wastes none of the flour, as does yeast, but it has its own disadvantages. The product of these chemicals acting on each other is a salt which is left in the bread; hydrochloric acid acted on by soda gives common salt, to which there could be no objection, but this method is not easily used in the household, and the salts left by other acids, as the lactic acid of milk when acted on by bicarbonate of soda, we get enough of in other dishes. Whether reliable experiments have been made as to the comparative digestibility of breads raised with soda and those raised with yeast the writer does not know, but there is a wide-spread impression that the former should be eaten only occasionally, and it is certain that we tire of them sooner than of yeast breads. Besides, which is of importance to one who must economize in milk, eggs, &c., better materials must be used with soda than with yeast to produce an equally rich tasting bread or cake.

METHODS.

We have three methods of using bicarbonate of soda to raise flour; by its action on

1. The acid contained in sour milk, from 1 to 2 teaspoons of soda being used to a quart of milk.

2. On cream of tartar, the proportions being 1 teaspoon soda to 2 of cream of tartar to a quart of flour.

3. On tartaric or other acids already mixed with it in a baking powder and to be used according to directions on the package, or, one may say in general, that three teaspoons of the powder go to every quart of flour.

Secret of Success. The secret of success in making soda raised breads consists in (1) the perfect mixing of the soda and cream of tartar or the baking powder, with the flour, cooks who are particular sieving these ingredients five times. In this connection we cannot urge too strongly that each housewife should make and keep on hand this prepared flour; in a leisure time she can measure, sieve and mix it, and she has then in making biscuit or cake, only to chop in the butter, add the milk and eggs and it is done.

2. In light mixing of the shortening with the flour; this is best accomplished with a chopping knife.

3. In a rapid completion of the work after the two raising agencies have become wet and begun to work, and no delay in baking when all is ready.

Soda Biscuits.

Ingredients. 1 qt. of flour, 1 teaspoon salt, 1 tablespoon butter, or butter and lard, or butter and suet, 1 scant pint *sweet* milk or water with 1 teaspoon soda and two of cream of tartar, or three teaspoons of baking powder; *or*, 1 scant pint *sour* milk with 1 teaspoon soda and 1 teaspoon cream of tartar; if the milk be very sour omit the cream of tartar.

To make. In a chopping bowl stir all well together except the shortening and milk, then *chop* in the shortening which should be cold and hard, till all is fine and well mixed. Now add the milk a little at a time, still mixing with the chopping knife. Take out on the moulding board and roll out with as little mixing as possible.

This dough is often made richer, even 1 cup of butter to 1 qt. of flour being used, but so much as this can only be considered extravagant and unhealthful.

As Biscuit.

To use this dough. Roll 1 in. thick, cut with biscuit cutter and bake. To be eaten warm with butter.

As Graham Biscuits.

Use three parts graham flour to one of wheat and treat in same manner.

As Short Cake.

Roll ½ in. thick, fit into jelly cake tins and bake. When nicely browned, split and butter and pile up like toast.

For fruit short cake (see pages 108 and 109.)

SODA BREAD OF CORN MEAL.

Corn Bread, or Johnny Cake.

1. Plain.

1 cup sweet milk, 1 cup sour or buttermilk, or both of sour milk, 1 teaspoon salt, 1 teaspoon soda, 1 tablespoon butter or suet or lard, 3 cups Indian meal, and 1 of wheat flour, or all of Indian meal. Pour into a tin and bake 40 minutes.

2. Richer.

The same with an egg and ½ cup sugar added.

3. Very Nice.

No. 1, with the addition of 3 eggs, ½ cup sugar and ⅓ cup butter, 1 cup meal being omitted.

SODA RAISED BREAD — THIN.

Pancakes without Eggs.

1. Of Wheat Flour.

Ingredients. 1 qt. flour, 1 teaspoon salt, and 1 scant qt. sour milk, with 2 level teaspoons soda and the same of cream of tartar unless the milk is very sour, when omit the cream of tartar. Sweet milk can also be used with 1 teaspoon soda and 2 of cream of tartar, or 3 of baking powder.

To make. Mix the salt and cream of tartar if used, with the flour. Make a hole in the middle and pour in the milk gradually, stirring with a spoon till smooth. Then beat hard for 5 minutes, or till it is bubbly. Add the soda dissolved in a teaspoon of hot water, and bake immediately on a very hot griddle.

Unless well beaten before the soda is added, these pancakes without eggs are not a success.

If made with sour milk they will be still better, if when mixed (without the soda, of course) the batter is left to stand twelve or even twenty-four hours.

Just before using add the soda dissolved in a little hot water.

2. Of Graham Flour. Are made in the same way, 1 part being of white flour and 3 parts graham.

3. Of Corn Meal. As above, with corn meal instead of graham.

Pancakes with Eggs.

Ingredients. To any of the 3 preceding recipes add 2 or 3 eggs, beating yolks and whites separately.

Muffins and Waffles.

Muffins and waffles of all kinds are the same as pancakes, made a little thicker and with the addition of 1 tablespoon of butter.

Fritters.

For fritters, which should be next in order (see page 113).

USES FOR BREAD.

These are so numerous that the housekeeper need never fear the accumulation of stale bread, if she will only take care of it in time. Every day the bits left

To Dry Bread. from meals and the dry ends of the loaf must be dried hard in the oven and then put away in paper bags. If time allows, pare off the crusts, cut into cubes and dry separately to add to soups.

This dried bread will keep for weeks or months — it must simply be kept clean and dry. In any recipe where bread-crumbs are called for, as bread pudding or bread omelet, use this dried bread, laying it first in *cold* water till it is soft, then pressing it dry in a towel and crumbling it lightly with the hand.

Here are a few of the ways in which bread can be used.

USES FOR BREAD IN SLICES.

Toast. In dry toast, milk toast, and water toast, to be eaten as such and as a foundation for many other dishes.

Fried toast — bread slices soaked in egg and milk, or water, and fried on a griddle with a little fat. (See page 60). Cold milk or water toast may be so used.

Fritters. For Bread Fritters (see page 114).

Puddings. For bread and butter pudding (see page 111).

Steamed Bread. Stale bread may be cut in slices and steamed so as to taste sweet and good. Set the slices up on end in the steamer and steam 5 or 10 minutes, then dry a little in an oven.

Bread Rebaked. Biscuits of all sorts, even when several days old, may be made nearly as good as when fresh, by wetting the tops and setting in a hot oven for about five minutes. A convenient way of having warm biscuits for breakfast.

USES FOR CRUMBS OR DRIED BREAD.

Soaked and crumbled as described on page 105 and use in bread dough instead of half the flour.

In bread omelettes (see page 60).

In meat balls for soups and stews (see page 127).

In bread dressing. Pour enough hot water on dry bread to soften it and chop it not too fine; season with chopped onion, herbs and suet or tried out fat. The addition of an egg is an improvement. Bake covered, about an hour, then uncover and brown. This mixture may also be used for stuffing a fowl, leg of mutton, &c.; or it may be fried in spoonfuls on a griddle and eaten with a sweet sauce as the simplest form of pancakes.

In bread pancakes (see page 93).

In bread puddings (see pages 109, 110 and 111).

For breading chops, croquettes, &c., that are to be fried in boiling fat.

SIMPLE SWEET DISHES.

This department does not pretend to be complete, it simply aims to classify as many of the cheaper kinds as the ordinary family needs. These will generally be used as desserts but there is no reason why the main dish of the meal should not have some sugar in it. I remember that in a simple *pension* in Thuringia, Germany, I once ate of a dinner consisting of a soup, a salad and one other dish, which we would call a bread pudding. I was helped bountifully to this main dish of the meal, I ate and was satisfied, for the materials were good and it was well made and delicately baked. The recipe will be found on page 110.

MILK PUDDINGS.

Indian pudding. 1 qt. of milk, ½ cup corn meal, 1 teaspoon salt, ½ cup chopped suet, 1 tablespoon ginger, ½ cup molasses. Bake covered for 3 hours in very slow oven and serve with sweet sauce.

Swelled rice pudding. 1 qt. skim milk or 1 pt. full milk and 1 pt. water, ½ cup rice, 2 tablespoons sugar, ½ teaspoon salt. Bake slowly 2 hours covered, then uncover and brown. It will be a creamy mass and delicious in taste. Serve without sauce. Raisins may be added.

Minute pudding of wheat or graham flour. *Ingredients.* 1 qt. milk — skim milk with 1 teaspoon butter will do — 2 eggs, ¾ pt. flour, 1 teaspoon salt. To prevent burning make in double boiler or pail set in a kettle of boiling water. Mix the flour and egg smooth with part of the milk, heat the remainder to boiling and stir in the egg and flour. Stir till it thickens, then let it swell and cook slowly for 15 minutes. Serve with fruit, or with sugar and milk.

Farina pudding. *Ingredients.* 1 pt. water, 1 pt. milk, 1 teaspoon salt, ½ pt. farina, 2 eggs. Make as above.

This is excellent cut in slices when cold and fried brown on a griddle. It may also be made without eggs.

Buttermilk pudding. *Ingredients.* 1 pt. fresh buttermilk, 2 tablespoons cream or butter, 1 teaspoon salt, a pinch of soda, and flour for stiff batter. Steam 2 hours, or till it bursts open, or bake in little cups or patties. May be eaten with any fruit sauce or with milk and sugar.

FRUIT PUDDINGS WITH SODA BISCUIT DOUGH.

Strawberry Shortcakes. For this dough, see page 102.

When baked as short cake, split the cakes and spread between each pair strawberries mashed and sweetened.

Other fruit shortcakes. In the same way make shortcake of berries of any sort, stewed apples, stewed pieplant, lemon or orange tart filling, in short, any filling for a pie, that is ready to eat without further cooking. These should be eaten warm but not hot, and are as good next day, if put in the oven long enough to become again warm and crisp.

Roly Poly pudding and apple dumpling. These favorite dishes are but modifications of the fruit shortcake. In the first the dough is made just stiff enough to roll out, covered with apples or berries or other fruit, then rolled up and put to bake in a pan containing a little water.

For apple dumplings, the crust is cut in squares, sliced apples placed in the middle, then the corners gathered up and pinched together. Bake like Roly Poly pudding, or steam.

Apple pie. If you wish to cook your fruit at the same time with the crust, fill a deep pie plate with fruit, as apples, and cover with the rolled out shortcake. Bake brown, and when done lift the crust, sweeten the fruit, replace the crust, and the "pie" is ready to serve.

Raised biscuit or bun dough (see page 98), can be used in the same way, or still better, yeast pancake mixture (see page 99), in layers with any sort of fruit.

If you will call these fruit shortcakes "pies," and be content therewith, you will save much labor, much expensive material, and set before your family a more healthful dish. No farther recipes for pies will be given; a few that are generally classed as such, coming more naturally under the head of puddings.

FRUIT PUDDINGS WITH BREAD.

1. Brown Betty. *Ingredients.* 1 pt. bread crumbs, or dry bread moistened, 1 qt. chopped sour apples, ½ pt. sugar, 2 teaspoons cinnamon, 4 tablespoons butter or suet.

Arrange bread and apples in layers in a pudding dish, beginning and ending with the bread crumbs, seasoning each layer with the sugar and spice and spreading the butter over the top. Cover it till the apples are soft, then uncover to brown.

2. Berry Betty. The same, made with raspberries or blackberries. If not juicy enough, a little water must be added. A pudding may be made in the same way with cherries or any other well flavored fruit.

CUSTARD PUDDINGS.

1. Plain. *Ingredients.* 1 qt. milk, 4 eggs, beaten yolks and whites separately, 4 tablespoons sugar, a grating of nutmeg and a pinch of salt. Bake in a buttered pudding dish till solid, and take from the oven before it curdles.

2. Rice and custard. To above ingredients add ½ cup of rice cooked soft in part of the milk, or in water. Bake ½ to ¾ of an hour, till nicely browned.

This is the foundation for the many varieties of rice puddings. Raisins may be added.

3. Tapioca. 4. Sago. Tapioca and Sago puddings are made in the same way, except that they must be soaked for 2 hours in part of the milk or in water.

Indian and custard pudding. To the ingredients for plain custard pudding add 1 pt. of corn meal and an extra cup of milk, 1 teaspoon salt, 1 teaspoon ginger, ¼ cup sugar and ½ cup chopped beef suet or 2 tablespoonfuls tried out fat. Scald the meal first in the milk and bake the pudding, covered, two hours in slow oven.

BREAD AND CUSTARD PUDDINGS.

1. Bread pudding or "Semmel Geraüsch." 1 qt. boiling milk poured on as much bread—as will absorb it, about 1 pt. if hard—4 eggs, ½ teaspoon salt, ½ cup sugar.

The milk and bread are allowed to get cold and the other ingredients well beaten with it, the eggs being beaten separately, and the whites added last. Bake one hour in a buttered dish. Eat without a sauce.

Of course a bread pudding can be made with fewer eggs, but then it will hardly do for the main dish of a meal.

2. Bread pudding (simple). Dried bread soaked soft in cold water and pressed dry in a cloth, milk to make it into a soft mush. Add 1 beaten egg to a pint of the mixture. Bake from half an hour to an hour and eat with sweet sauce.

With raisins. Raisins or currants or fresh fruit, as cherries, may be added.

With dried apples. After putting in ½ the pudding mixture, put a thick layer of stewed dried apples mashed and sweetened, and flavored with orange peel or cinnamon.

Bread and butter pudding. A convenient variation on the ordinary bread pudding.

Plain. Spread thin slices of bread with butter, and pour over them a simple custard, viz.: 4 eggs to 1 qt. of milk, 4 tablespoons sugar, a pinch of salt. Keep pressed down till the custard is absorbed; Bake slowly till firm and brown. Eat with or without sauce.

With fruit. The bread slices may be spread with India currants, or with any kind of fresh or dried cooked fruit, not too juicy.

Individual bread puddings. Cut small round loaves of bread into quarters, or use biscuits. Soak in a mixture of 4 eggs, whites and yolks, beaten separately, and added to 1 pt. of milk with a little sugar and nutmeg. When they have absorbed all they will without breaking, drain and bake in slow oven to a nice brown, spreading a little butter over once or twice at the last. This dish can be made very pretty by putting currants in the holes around the top and sticking in pieces of blanched almonds.

SUET PUDDINGS.

Ingredients. ½ pt. beef suet, chopped fine, ½ pt. molasses, ½ pt. milk, ½ pt. raisins or currants, or both. (A part of the fruit may be figs and prunes cut in bits.) 1 teaspoon salt, 1 teaspoon soda mixed with the molasses, 1 pt. bread crumbs (dry), 1 pt. graham flour and 2 eggs. Steam 3 hours or bake 2.

Eat with a lemon sauce.

Simple. Use the above recipe, omitting the eggs and using instead of graham flour and bread crumbs 1¾ pt. white flour.

To reheat puddings. All the preceding puddings are good reheated. Cut in slices, and warm in the oven, or fry in a little butter in a pan. Sift sugar over and eat with sauce.

PUDDING SAUCE.

1 pt. water made into a smooth starch with a heaping tablespoon flour. Cook 10 minutes, strain if necessary, sweeten to taste and pour it on 1 tablespoon butter and juice of a lemon or other flavoring. If lemon is not used add 1 tablespoon vinegar.

This can be made richer by using more butter and sugar; stir them to a cream with the flavoring, then add the starch.

FRITTERS.

These are various doughs and batters fried in boiling fat, and eaten warm with sugar or a sweet sauce. The hot fat gives a puffy lightness and a delicious crisp crust.

Lard is most generally used, but cooking oil (see page 41) is better, and even beef fat prepared as (see same page) is good. The fat must be smoking hot to prevent its soaking into the dough. For the same reason batters so cooked must contain more egg than if they were to be baked.

Forms. The fritter may be rolled out and cut in shapes, or dropped in spoonfuls or run through a funnel, being, of course, mixed of different consistency for each method. When nicely browned, take out with a wire spoon and lay on brown paper, which will absorb the fat, then sprinkle with sugar and send to table.

Soda raised fritters. *Ingredients.* 1 pt. flour (½ may be graham), ½ teaspoon salt, 1 teaspoon oil, butter, or lard, 1 egg and ½ pt. sour milk with ½ teaspoon soda, or same of sweet milk with ½ teaspoon soda and 1 teaspoon cream of tartar. Beat the egg, white and yolk separately, adding the white last of all.

Drop from a spoon into boiling lard; *or*, omit nearly half the flour and pour through a funnel.

This batter may be also raised with yeast.

Egg raised fritters. These are more crisp and delicate. If liked very light, soda or cream of tartar or baking powder may be added to these also. These batters are thinner than the preceding; they must be well beaten if no soda is used.

10

1. *Ingredients.* 1 scant pt. of flour, 2 eggs, 1 teaspoon salt, ½ pt. milk, 1 teaspoon oil or butter.

Beat the yolks well, then again well with the flour and milk, add the stiffly beaten whites last. Fry in spoonfuls.

2. *Ingredients.* 1 heaping pt. flour, 4 eggs, 1 tablespoon oil or butter, 1 teaspoon salt, about a pint of water, or enough to make the batter a little thicker than for pancakes. Proceed as before.

Additions. 1 tablespoon of lemon juice may be added to any of the above recipes, or a little nutmeg or cinnamon if liked.

Fruit fritters. Take sour apples, peel, cut out the core neatly and slice round in slices ¼ in. thick. Soak these a few hours in sweetened wine, lemon juice or other flavoring. Dip in either of the above batters and fry. (They are also very good without being soaked in the flavoring.)

Peaches, pine apples and bananas may be used in the same way.

Bread fritters. Trim the crust from sliced bread, cut in nice shapes and soak soft, but not till they break, in a cup of milk to which has been added 1 beaten egg and some flavoring, as cinnamon, lemon, etc. Dip in fritter batter and fry.

COOKING OF VEGETABLES.

The Legumes. As we have seen, the food value of the dried bean, pea and lentil, is great, but as usually cooked a large per cent. of it is lost to us.

In the process of cooking, the cellulose part must be broken up, softened, and as much as possible entirely removed. These vegetables, if they cannot be obtained ground, must be soaked in cold water some time before cooking, cooked till very soft and then mashed and sieved. No form of cooking that does not include sieving can be recommended except for very hardy stomachs. See pages 55 and 117.

Potato. This vegetable must also be treated with care. The starch grains of which it is so largely composed swell in the process of cooking, and burst the cellulose walls confining them, but when this stage is reached the potato is too often spoiled by being allowed to absorb steam and become sodden. As soon as tender, boiled potatoes should be drained, dried out a few moments, then sprinkled with salt, and the kettle covered close with a towel, until they are served. They should then be put into a napkin and sent to the table.

Other vegetables. Other garden vegetables are cooked more or less alike; put into boiling water and kept at a rapid boil until tender, and no longer,—the length of time varying for any given vegetable according to the freshness, size, and degree of maturity. When done or nearly so, they should be seasoned and served as soon as possible.

Mixed vegetables.

A welcome variety in the serving of vegetables can be found in skillful mixture of two or more kinds. A few of these mixtures are, green corn and shelled beans, or succotash, green corn and tomatoes, green corn with stewed potatoes, potatoes and turnips mashed together, green peas with a quarter as many carrots cut very small, potatoes with same proportion of carrots and seasoned with fried sliced onions poured over.

Vegetables and fruits.

There are also mixtures of vegetables and fruits that are very successful, as lentils or beans with a border of stewed prunes.

SOUPS WITHOUT MEAT.

In general. These soups should be largely used by the economical housewife; they are cheap and nutritious, and if carefully made and seasoned, excellent in taste. A large number of recipes are given, from which can be selected what is suited to materials on hand, to amount of time and quantity of fire.

These will be arranged under Vegetable Soups, Flour and Bread Soups, and Cold Soups.

VEGETABLE SOUPS.

If any meat bones are on hand or trimmings of meat not otherwise needed, simmer them from one to two hours in water and use the broth thus obtained instead of water in making any of the following soups.

Most important are those made from the dried bean, pea and lentil, the three pod-covered vegetables. For their nutritive qualities see page 81.

Bean soup.

Ingredients. 1 lb. beans, 1 onion, 2 tablespoons beef fat, salt and pepper.

Additions, to be made according to taste. ¼ lb. pork, or a ham bone, a pinch of red pepper, or, an hour before serving, different vegetables, as carrots and turnips, chopped and fried.

Soak the beans over night in 2 qts. water. In the morning pour off, put on fresh water and cook with the onion and fat till very soft, then mash or press through a cullender to remove the skins, and add enough water to make 2 qts. of somewhat thick soup. Season.

This soup may also be made from cold baked beans. Boil ½ hr., or till they fall to pieces, then strain and season.

Split or dried pea soup. Make like bean soup.

Lentil soup. Make like bean soup.

Green Vegetable Soups. The water in which vegetables have been cooked should **never** be thrown away, with the exception of that used for cooking beets, and potatoes boiled without peeling; even cabbage water can be made the basis of a good soup.

General method. Boil the vegetables until very tender, mash or press through a cullender, thin sufficiently and season.

Potato soup. Good and cheap.

Ingredients. 6 large potatoes peeled, 1 large onion, 1 heaping teaspoon salt, ¼ teaspoon pepper. For a richer soup add ¼ lb. salt pork cut in bits (in this case put in less salt) or add 1 cup of milk or a beaten egg. Chopped celery leaves give a good flavor.

Boil potatoes, onions and salt in a little water, and when very soft mash; then add, a little at a time and stirring to keep it smooth, a qt. of hot water and 1 tablespoon beef fat in which 1 tablespoon flour has been cooked; *or* use the fat for frying bread dice, which add at the last minute.

Most cooks fry the sliced onion before putting it in the soup, but the difference in taste is so slight as not to be worth the few minutes extra time, if time is an object.

Green pea soup. This is a delicious soup and very nutritious. Large peas, a little too hard to be used as a vegetable, may be utilized in its manufacture.

Ingredients. 1 pt. shelled peas, 3 pts. water, 1 small onion, 1 tablespoon butter or fat, 1 tablespoon flour. Salt and pepper.

Put peas and onion in boiling water and cook ½ an hour to an hour, till very soft. Press through cullender and season.

Pea and tomato soup. Add to above when done, 1 pt. stewed tomatoes and a little more seasoning. This is an excellent soup, having the nutrition of the pea and the flavor of the tomato.

Tomato soup. Valuable for its fine flavor, and may be made nutritious also by adding broth, milk or eggs.

Ingredients. 1 pt. tomatoes, 2 pts. water, 1 tablespoon fat, 1 tablespoon flour, salt and pepper.

Cook the flour in the fat, add the peeled tomatoes and a very little water. When they have cooked to pieces, mash them against the side of the pot, add the rest of the water and the seasoning.

Tomato soup No. 2. Proceed as above, using instead of half the water, 1 pt. of milk, into which ¼ tea spoon soda has been stirred.

Parsnip soup. *Ingredients.* 1 pt. of parsnips cut in pieces, 3 small potatoes, 3 pts. water, or water and milk, salt, pepper and butter.

Cook till the vegetables fall to pieces, mash and add

seasoning. If milk can be substituted for part of the water the soup will be improved.

Young vegetable or spring soup. *Ingredients.* 1 pt. chopped onion, carrot, turnips and celery root in about equal parts, 1 tablespoon fat, 1 teaspoon sugar, salt and pepper.

Heat the fat, add sugar, salt and pepper, then stir the vegetables in it till they begin to brown, add 3 pts. water and set back to simmer 1 to 2 hours. Serve without straining.

Green corn soup. *Ingredients.* ½ doz. ears green corn, 3 pts. water, 1 tablespoon fat and 1 tablespoon flour salt and pepper, an egg and a cup of milk.

Cut the corn from the cob and boil one hour. Add the flour which has been fried in the fat, season and strain.

Dried corn soup. Make as above, using dried corn, soaked over night and boiled 2 hours.

Sorrel soup. An excellent flavor, new to most of us.

Ingredients. 1 pt. sheep's sorrel, light measure (bought in city markets, or gathered in country fields), 1 onion, a few leaves of lettuce and parsley all chopped fine, ⅛ teaspoon nutmeg, 1 tablespoon fat, 2 tablespoons flour, 3 pts. water, 1 or 2 eggs, 1 cup milk, salt and pepper.

Heat the fat, add the chopped vegetables and sweat or steam for 10 minutes, then add flour and last the boiling water; add the milk just before serving. Serve fried bread with it.

"Hit and Miss" soup. To illustrate how all bits can be used, here is a soup actually made from "leavings."

1 cup water drained from macaroni, 1 cup water drained from cabbage, with a few shreds of the cabbage, 2 small bones from roast veal, 1 scant tablespoon boiled rice. Simmer these together with a chopped onion while the rest of the dinner is cooking, thicken with a little flour and serve with fried bread.

FLOUR AND BREAD SOUPS.

Flour soup. *Ingredients.* 1 tablespoon beef fat, 1 heaping tablespoon flour, 2 sliced onions, 2 pts. water, 1 pt. milk, 1 cupful of mashed potato, salt and pepper.

Fry the onions in the fat until light brown; remove, pressing out the fat. In same fat now cook the flour till it is yellow, and add, a little at a time, the water. Put back the onions and let it stand awhile, then add milk and potato. Salt well.

The potato may be omitted and a little more flour used.

Browned Flour soup. *Ingredients.* 1 tablespoon butter or fat, ½ cup flour, 2 pts. water, 1 pt. milk, 1 teaspoon salt.

Cook the flour brown in the fat over a slow fire or in the oven; add slowly the water and other ingredients. Serve with fried bread.

Browned Farina soup. Make like above, but of wheat farina.

Bread soup. *Ingredients.* Dry bread, broken in bits, water, salt and pepper, an onion and a little fat.

Soak the bread in boiling water for a few minutes, add the onion sliced and fried in the fat; salt and pepper well.

Or, use milk instead of water, and toasted or fried bread.

Noodle Soup. (See page 91.)

MILK SOUPS OR PORRIDGES.

These are especially good in families where there are children, and would be welcome on almost any supper table. They are almost equally good eaten cold.

In making, use a porcelain kettle or an iron kettle, greasing it first with a little fat, as a scorched taste spoils the dish.

Wheat Porridge (salted.) *Ingredients.* 3 pts. milk, 1 pt. of water (or half water and half milk), $\frac{1}{3}$ cup flour, 2 eggs, 2 teaspoons salt.

To the boiling milk and water, add the flour stirred smooth with a little cold milk; let it cook 10 minutes. Beat the eggs in gradually, but do not cook them; serve with fried bread. Grated cheese is an addition to this soup.

Wheat Porridge (sweet.) Same as above, but using only a pinch of salt, and as flavoring 3 tablespoons sugar and $\frac{1}{4}$ teaspoon cinnamon. The flavor may be varied by using grated lemon peel, nutmeg, vanilla, bitter almond or 2 fresh peach leaves boiled with the milk.

Of Farina. These two porridges are still better made of farina instead of flour.

Barley Porridge. Pearl barley is soaked over night in water, and then cooked for 2 hours till soft. During the last hour add milk instead of water, as it dries away. Flavor with salt and butter.

Indian Meal Porridge. *Ingredients.* 1 cup meal, 2 qts. water, 1 tablespoon flour, 1 pt. milk, salt, and a little ginger (if liked). Boil the meal and water an hour; add flour and salt and boil ¼ hour, and add the milk just before serving.

Oatmeal Porridge. Make in the same way, using oatmeal instead of flour.

Graham Porridge. 1 cup graham flour to 3 pts. milk and water. Cook 15 minutes. This may be varied in flavor like flour porridge.

These three Porridges can be made from cold corn, oatmeal or graham mush.

Chocolate Soup. *Ingredients.* ¼ lb. chocolate, 2½ qts. milk and water, sugar to taste, 1 egg yolk, a little vanilla or cinnamon.

Cook the chocolate soft in a little water and add the rest; when boiling put in the other ingredients and cook the beaten white of an egg in spoonfuls on the top. Serve with fried bread.

Buttermilk Soup or "Pop." The foreign kitchen has many recipes for this soup quite unknown among us. Cooking brings out the acid, but once used to that taste, one finds the soup good and wholesome.

Ingredients. To each pt. of buttermilk, 1 tablespoon flour and 1 tablespoon butter, a little salt.

Bring gradually to a boil, stirring constantly to prevent curdling, and pour on fried bread.

Varieties. Sugar and cinnamon are often added to this soup; also the yolk and beaten white of 1 egg. It is considered nutritious for the sick.

Another. The Germans often add to this soup small potatoes, and bits of fried bacon. In which case the butter is omitted.

Or to the buttermilk soup when done, is added half the quantity of cooked pears or prunes.

Brewis. To salted boiling milk, put enough bread crumbs (either white or graham) to make a thick smooth porridge.

Sour Cream Soup. This soup is earnestly recommended for trial, as there are few ways in which such a delicious taste may be given to simple materails.

Ingredients. 3 pts. water, ½ cup sour cream and the following mixture: ¼ cup milk, ½ cup flour, 1 teaspoon butter, ½ tablespoon salt, 1 teaspoon sugar, 1 egg, 1 tablespoon fluid yeast or ¼ teaspoon compressed yeast. Mix these together into a dough and let it get light, then drop half of it in teaspoonfuls into the boiling water and cream; then thin the rest with water until it will pour, add it to the soup and cook 5 minutes. (Not all the dough may be needed.)

Cider soup. *Ingredients.* 1 pt. cider just beginning to work, 1 pt. water, 1 cup milk (boiling), 1 tablespoon flour, a little cinnamon and sugar.

Let cider and water come to a boil, add the flour rubbed smooth, and cook a few minutes; and lastly add the milk. Serve with toast. An egg yolk may be added.

FRUIT SOUPS.

To be eaten Warm or Cold.

These are made of almost any well flavored fruit, cooked soft and mashed, sufficient water added, with a little thickening, sugar and spice. They are especially welcome in summer; may be eaten as a first course, or set aside to be used as a drink during the meal.

Apple soup, No. 1. *Ingredients.* 4 cups peeled and quartered apples, cooked to a mush in a little water, 1½ pts. water, 1 teaspoon cornstarch, 3 teaspoons sugar, ¼ teaspoon cinnamon, a pinch of salt.

No. 2. A soup plate full apples, 1 cup of rice. Cook soft and rub through a sieve, adding a little sugar, cinnamon, lemon peel, and an egg yolk. Thin sufficiently with water.

No. 3. Instead of rice, use in the above recipe bread with the addition of a few India currants.

No. 4. Instead of rice, use oatmeal and cook till soft, or use that already cooked.

Plum Soup. Make like apple soup, but if the plums are very sour add a little soda, —¼ teaspoon to a qt. of soup.

Cherry Soup. Made in the same manner.

These soups may also be made of dried plums, prunes or dried sour cherries. Soak the fruit over night.

Soups of Pears, etc., If soup is made of a milder fruit, as pears, which are at some seasons so cheap, add a few sour apples or more spice, to give flavor.

ADDITIONS TO SOUPS.

If your soup has not strength enough, milk and eggs may be added if no meat stock is at hand.

How to add eggs. The egg should be beaten, mixed with a little of the soup, then added to the rest, but not boiled. The yolk is better for this purpose than the white.

Meat Extract. Liebig's meat extract is very valuable for adding flavor to a soup but it is too expensive for general use.

1. Flour. This may be boiled a few minutes with the soup after being mixed smooth in a little water, or better, cook it in a little butter or melted beef fat before adding to the soup.

2. Bread Sponge. On baking day, save a little of the bread sponge, make thin enough to pour, and if you wish, add a beaten egg. Set away half an hour to rise again, and when light pour into the soup.

3. Farina. This preparation of wheat, now sold by the pound at a reasonable price, is most valuable as an addition to soup; it needs only to be sprinkled in and boiled for a few moments.

4. Potato. Mashed potato mixed smooth with a little milk or grated cold potato may be added to soup to give body.

5. Barley. Add to the soup 1 hour before it is done pearl barley that has been soaked over night.

6. Rice. One-half hour before serving, add to soup 1 tablespoon of rice to a quart of soup.

7. Bread. Bits of bread dried hard in the oven, may be added to the soup just before serving, *or* fry them in the spider in a little beef fat, *or* soak in milk and egg before frying. *Or*, toast bread and cut in squares.

8. Vegetables. Any small vegetables may be added, such as asparagus tops, tiny onions that have been first boiled in another pot, cooked peas, beans, etc. A favorite Russian soup is beef soup, with the addition of beets, cabbage and carrots.

Most important of all additions to soup are those which need a little more time to prepare, but are worth the trouble if the soup is to be the principal part of the dinner. Such are the following:

DUMPLINGS FOR SOUPS AND STEWS.

This word has an unpleasant sound, too suggestive of the heavy and unwholesome balls often served under this name, but there seems to be no other name under which these different preparations can be classed. Their basis is bread and eggs, or flour and eggs.

Bread mentioned here is hard dried bread ; it must be softened by soaking in *cold* water (hot water makes it pasty), then press it dry in a cloth and crumble it.

Meat Balls. Any cooked meat or several different kinds when there is too little of each to be otherwise used, is chopped fine and mixed with as much bread, salted and peppered, a little chopped suet or butter, or better still, marrow, and a chopped onion and some herbs, and to each cup of this mixture allow an egg. Mix lightly, make out into little balls and cook in very gently boiling soup. Try one first to see if it holds together. If not, add a little flour.

Fish balls. Substitute for the meat any cooked fish, chopped fine.

Marrow balls. Two eggs to 1 cup of bread and marrow size of an egg, chopped. Make as above.

Bacon Balls. Instead of marrow, add cubes of bacon fried brown.

All these mixtures can also be fried in a pan as an omelette, or baked.

Flour and Bread Balls. Three cups, half bread, half flour, 1 egg, butter size of an egg, 1 cup milk and water, salt. Soak the bread in the milk and water, and make out into little balls with the other ingredients. Cook, covered, 15 minutes (may also be boiled in salted water and eaten with fruit).

Egg Sponge. One egg, 1 teaspoon flour, a little salt. Beat white of egg to foam, mix lightly with the rest and pour on top of the soup. Turn over in a few minutes with a skimmer, and before putting into the turreen, cut it in pieces.

No. 2. 1 heaping tablespoon flour to 1 egg and the yolk of another, and 1 teaspoon butter. Beat hard and drop in with a teaspoon.

Schwaben Spetzel. One egg, 3 tablespoons milk, nearly ½ cup of flour, salt. Pour through a funnel into soup or into salted water, cook 5 minutes and use to garnish beef.

Biscuit Dough Balls. An excellent addition to a stew or soup is of biscuit or rusk dough (see page 98), made into balls no larger than a chestnut, and cooked in the stew, or steamed in a cloth above it.

Buttermilk Balls. Also the following of buttermilk: 1 cup buttermilk, ½ teaspoon of soda, 1 egg, salt, and flour enough to allow of the batter being dropped in spoonfuls.

Macaroni. Cooked macaroni cut in pieces an inch long, is a pleasant addition to soup.

FLAVORS OR SEASONINGS.

Without doubt "hunger is the best sauce," but it is not true, as many think, that a craving for variety is the sign of a pampered and unnatural appetite; even animals, whom we cannot accuse of having "notions," have been known to starve in the experimenter's hands rather than eat a perfectly nutritious food of whose flavor they had wearied, and prisoners become so tired of a too oft repeated dish that they vomit at the sight and smell of it.

What we call flavors may or may not be associated with a real food. Meats are rich in flavors and each fruit has its peculiar taste; then, there are the spices and aromatic herbs which are not parts of a real food, and it is most important that the cook should understand the art of adding these as seasonings to mild tasting foods, so as to make new dishes which shall be both nutritious and appetizing. The bulk of our nourishment must be made up of the flesh of a few animals, a half-dozen grains and as many garden vegetables, but the skillful cook can make of them, with the help of other flavors, an endless variety of dishes.

An American traveling on the continent of Europe becomes acquainted with many new dishes and tastes, and although not all of them are to his liking, he must conclude that our cookery, compared for instance, with that of the French, is very monotonous. To be sure, we have the advantage of the European in that our markets offer us a greater variety of natural foods, especially fruits, each having a flavor of its own, and this fact makes us somewhat more independent of the art of the cook; but still we have need for every lesson of this sort, and especially is this the case with the poor, who must keep to the cheapest food materials, which are not in themselves rich in flavor.

Spices and other flavors, when not used to excess, stimulate our digestive organs to appropriate more easily the food to which they are added; their agreeable odor starts the digestive juices, both in the mouth and in the stomach, and their flavor acting on the palate has the same effect.

The more common spices and flavors, as the housewife uses these terms, are salt, pepper, mustard, cinnamon and mace, nutmegs, cloves, ginger, caraway and coriander seeds, vanilla, and many volatile oils, such as those contained in the rind of lemons and oranges; and to this list we must add certain vegetables, as the horseradish and various members of the onion family, the caper and nasturtium seeds, and the aromatic herbs.

All these have their use and their abuse. Salt is hardly thought of in this list, so necessary do we consider it, and its use is well enough governed by our palate, though no doubt we over, rather than under salt our foods. Pepper is also in nearly every household used to excess, being added to too many dishes. The pungent mustard should be still more carefully used; but a little of it adds relish to a salad or a meat sauce, and goes especially well with certain vegetables, as beans. Cinnamon, mace and nutmeg, we use principally with sweet dishes, but nutmeg makes a nice variety in certain meat stews and in croquettes; foreign cooks use it far too much to suit our taste. Almost our only use of the caraway and coriander seeds is in cookies; try the former in a potato soup for variety. Ginger seems to go well with Indian meal in a pudding or porridge, and with molasses, wherever used.

To give the uses for onions and for the aromatic herbs would be too long a task. The latter can all be bought in a dried state very cheaply, and they retain their flavor well; one of the most useful, however, parsley, is much better fresh; by all means keep a little box of it growing in a window. Perhaps, after onion, celery is most useful as a flavor for soups and stews, root, stem, leaves and seeds being all valuable.

In the flavoring of soups and stews, it is well to use a number of flavors, letting no one of them be prominent above the others; on the other hand, it is well to have certain favorite dishes seasoned always in the same way; as fresh pork with sage; summer savory in a bread dressing, etc.

DRINKS AT MEALS.

A warm drink at meals is better than a cold one, especially in winter or at any time when we are tired; and the drinking of ice water cannot be too strongly condemned, lowering as it does the temperature of the stomach and so delaying digestion. To furnish warm drinks for each meal, acceptable to the palate, cheap and harmless, is no easy question. Soups or broth once adopted as a part of two meals in the day, as is so frequently seen in Europe, and the problem is half solved; indeed some of the drinks here given are really thin vegetable soups or porridges to which the flavor of salt or of sugar may be given according to taste.

Coffee.

It may be concluded, after comparing authors on the subject, that although coffee somewhat retards digestion and acts as a stimulant to the nervous system, still one or even two cups of moderately strong coffee a day will not harm a healthy person. We may say, therefore, that its use to this extent is a question of expense only.

Java and Mocha coffee in equal parts are considered the best mixture. Rio is much cheaper, and of strong, pure flavor. The amount to be used for moderately strong coffee is 1 tablespoon (ground) to a cup.

Chicory is considered here only as an adulterant, whereas in Europe a very little of it, say $\frac{1}{2}$ teaspoon of the prepared chicory to a cup of ground coffee, is used to improve the flavor.

Next to the quality of the coffee, it is of importance that it should be freshly ground and browned. If you buy it browned, reheat it first before grinding. The easiest and most economical way of making is to grind it very fine and put into a bag made of woven stuff, a white stocking top will do; leave room to swell. Heat this in your coffee pot as hot as you can without burning. Pour on boiling water and keep it hot and close-covered for 15 or 20 minutes.

Boiling coffee increases its strength, but does not improve its flavor.

Tea. All authors agree as to the harmfulness of strong tea, taken to excess.

Take great pains in making tea. Use an earthen teapot, and have a tea cozy or a large flannel cloth to wrap it in.

The water used should be between hard and soft, extracting the aroma but not the astringency; in China river water is used. If hard water must be used, remember that boiling increases its hardness and that it should be used as soon as it reaches the boiling point.

Take 1 teaspoonful of tea to a cup, put it in the teapot and heat in an oven till hot, pour on 1 cup of water that has just come to a boil, and cover with the tea cozy. Let it stand 5 minutes, then fill up with the requisite quantity of hot water and serve immediately.

Cocoa and chocolate. These both contain a good deal of nourishment, and as drinks are considered rather heavy. As the various kinds differ very much from each other, they are best prepared according to the recipes found on the packages.

"Cambric Tea." Milk, except for children, can hardly be looked upon as a drink, but diluted with hot water, and sweetened, it has already been christened for the children as "cambric tea," and it is no bad drink for their elders.

Gruels. A very thin gruel, slightly sweetened, is a good drink.

Oatmeal gruel. Into a qt. of boiling water stir 2 tablespoons oatmeal; boil for an hour or longer, strain through a coarse sieve or a cullender, add a pinch of salt, and a little milk and sugar.

Rice gruel. Wet 1 tablespoon rice flour in a little cold milk, put into 1 qt. boiling water, salt slightly and boil till transparent. Flavor with a little lemon peel and sugar.

Cornmeal gruel. 1 qt. boiling water, 3 tablespoons corn meal washed in several waters, ½ teaspoon salt; add ½ cup milk and a little sugar;—a pinch of ginger is an improvement.

Barley gruel. Soak pearl or ground barley all night or a few hours in cold water, put into boiling water and cook till very soft. Season like the others.

Sago and Tapioca gruel. Can be made in the same way.

All these drinks must be thin and not too highly seasoned.

Corn coffee Brown common field corn as you would coffee, as brown as you can without burning. Grind coarsely and steep like coffee. Add milk and sugar, and you will find it a delicious drink.

Cold drinks in Summer. Lemonade is too strongly acid for a regular drink at meals, but lemon as a flavor is always welcome.

Irish moss lemonade. Wash a handful of Irish moss in 5 waters, pour over it 2 qts. boiling water and let it stand till cold. Strain, adding more water if necessary and add the juice of 2 lemons and sweeten with lump sugar which you have rubbed on the lemons to obtain the oil in the skin.

Soda cream. 1 lb. sugar, 1 oz. tartaric acid dissolved in a pt. of hot water. When cold flavor with lemon zest or extract, and add the beaten white of an egg. When used, add 2 tablespoons of it to a glass of water in which you have dissolved ¼ teaspoon soda.

Apple water. Slice juicy sour apples into boiling water and keep warm an hour. Strain and sweeten. All these drinks taste best cooled (but not *too* cold) with ice.

Cider. Sweet cider can be bottled for use and makes a delicious drink. Boil and skim till it is clear—no longer; pour hot into bottles, and seal.

See also vegetable and fruit soups.

COOKERY FOR THE SICK.

It is comparatively easy for your family to live on a small income while all its members are in good health, but you will find your resources all too slender when you must cater for the appetite of an invalid.

At best, sickness is always a severe drain on the limited income, but here, as in every other department of your work, you will find that good sense and ingenuity will often stand you in stead for money.

During a severe illness the food as much as the medicine is under the care of the physician, but when the danger is over and he has left you with only general directions, you will be more than likely in your bewilderment to take the advice of the first neighbor that drops in, although you may know that neither her judgment nor experience is as good as your own.

Now consider first, what did the doctor mean by saying that the patient must be "built up," and how is the wasted frame to get back the fat and muscle that were burned away in the sickness? Chiefly, as you know, by the digestion of food, the proteids and fats and carbohydrates that we have been talking about, and still another, a real food although so often forgotten, the oxygen of the air.

We have said that we need not concern ourselves about this food, that it would take care of itself; and so it will when we are in a state of health and living

12

as human beings should, for as we walk or work we are fed by the air without knowing it. But the case is quite different with a poor invalid shut up in a sick room, we must bring the fresh air to him with as much care and regularity as we do his jellies and broths.

When we are considering what we shall feed our invalid, we cannot do better than keep to our old classification of Proteids, Fats, and Carbohydrates. He must have all these principles but in the most digestible form, for the stomach is feeble like the rest of the body. For this reason the proteids must be furnished mainly from the animal kingdom, butter and cream must supply the fat, and the carbohydrates must bring with them as little as possible of the tough cellulose, and they must be so cooked as to be easily digested.

First, as to the Proteids.

Hot milk, given often in small quantities, is much used in the early stages of recovery and is generally better liked if accompanied by a bit of toasted bread or made into a thin gruel.

In the first rank, also, comes soup made of lean beef scraped fine, covered with cold water and allowed to stand for an hour, then brought slowly to scalding heat and kept there for a short time; it is then strained through a coarse sieve, the small brown flakes being allowed to pass. Season only with salt. Or, broil a thick, tender steak, cut it in pieces, and then with a lemon squeezer press out every particle of juice, it may then be diluted and seasoned.

Mutton broth is made like beef soup but should be cooked a longer time. Chicken broth also requires more cooking.

Any of these soups may have a little rice or tapioca cooked with them.

Eggs are an important item in the diet of an invalid, being very nutritious and, if fresh, easily digested; do not use them at all if uncertain of their age.

Eggs may be given raw (see page 58) or soft-boiled (see page 59) or poached in hot water. An egg may be served in many ways and makes always a pretty and attractive dish. In cooking, it should never be submitted to a high temperature, as that makes the white part horny and indigestible.

A custard made from an egg and a cup of milk and a half table spoon of sugar may be given early in a convalescence. Or use beef soup or chicken broth instead of the milk, and flavor with a little salt and pepper. These custards should be made in a pail set in a kettle of boiling water, the custard being stirred till it begins to thicken.

Next in order, comes cooked meat. Beef is best of all, but let it be juicy and tender and broil or roast it, serving it rare. Probably a broiled mutton chop ranks next, although chicken, because of its delicate flavor will often receive the first choice. An invalid should not touch pork, and should be given veal or lamb only in the form of soup.

As to fats, the system needs them of course, but fat meat should not be given, only butter or better still, cream. The butter must never be melted and soaked into the food, nor made into a sauce.

As to the vegetable part of the diet, much care must be used. In the form of gruel or porridge, it is generally very welcome and gives the fluid part of the meal in a good form. For Indian meal and oatmeal porridge see page 122. Milk may take the place of the water.

Toast is with good reason considered invalids' food, for the process of toasting turns part of the starch of the bread into dextrine which is digested with great ease. Grains may be also browned or roasted. Roast rice as you would coffee, cook as usual and eat with a little cream. Remember that bread for toast must be cut thin and first dried out at a little distance from the fire, then brought nearer and browned. You may then serve it as dry toast lightly buttered, or in addition to the butter and a little salt, pour hot water or milk on it just before serving.

Panada of toasted brown bread, white bread or crackers, is made by piling the pieces in a bowl, having sprinkled either salt or sugar over, and then pouring over enough boiling water to soak them well. It should be kept hot for an hour or more, the pieces then lifted out carefully on a hot saucer and served with a little cream and perhaps more salt or sugar. Nutmeg may be added.

Rice is also a very valuable food for use in sickness, as it does not tax the most delicate digestion.

Macaroni is easily digested and of high food value. It should be boiled in salted hot water till tender and served with a little butter or cream. Or it may be added to a custard and lightly baked.

Barley, thoroughly cooked, is good food for an invalid. Oatmeal must be used with caution until the digestion becomes stronger.

As to vegetables proper, a mealy baked potatoe is

perhaps the first to be introduced into the bill of fare; remove the inside, mash fine and season with a little salt and cream. Beware of potatoes cooked in any other way.

The juice of fruits may be used early as a flavor in drinks, but the pulp must be discarded. A baked apple is safest to begin with, when the time comes to introduce fruit as such into the diet.

As to the serving, use the best china, silver and linen that you have in the house and let exquisite neatness never fail.

Remember that surprises are delightful to a sick person; never let the bill of fare be known before hand, and if you can disguise a well known dish, so much the better. Beaten white of egg is a good fairy and serves you cheaply. Snowy white or made golden brown in the oven, it may top many a dish, concealing at one time a custard, at another a mold of chicken jelly or even a cup of delicate apple sauce.

The processes of cooking, if simple, an invalid loves to watch and the sight is often a whet to the appetite. Bring his gruel to him in the form of mush and thin it before his eyes with milk or cream, coddle his egg in a stone ware bowl while he eats another course, and by all means make his tea at the bed-side.

BILLS OF FARE.

The following bills of fare are made out for a family of six persons, consisting of a working man, two women, and three children between the ages of six and fifteen, the size of the family and the ages attained being considered sufficiently near the average.

The amount of food and the proportions in which the great food principles are represented approximate to what is demanded by standard dietaries for such a family. For the man of the family we have taken, as has been said, the one proposed by Professor Atwater for an American at average manual labor, for the women and children those proposed by Prof. König.

Dietary adopted. The amounts represented by them are:

	Proteids.	Fats.	Carbohydrates.
Man	125 gms.	125 gms.	400 gms.
2 women (each)	96 "	48 "	400 "
3 children, 6 to 15 yrs. (each)	76 "	44 "	320 "
Sum total is	545 gms.	353 gms.	2210 gms.
Or translated into oz.	19.19 oz.	12.42 oz.	78.03 oz.

In calculating these amounts we have followed almost entirely the analytical tables compiled by Prof. König.

Meat is reckoned without bone and moderately fat, and in nearly all the bills of fare the amount of proteids enough exceeds that required by the dietary adopted so that we can afford this loss. Flour is of medium quality, eggs are reckoned without shell, and milk as weighing 34.4 oz. per qt.

As to prices, they are mainly those of Baltimore markets, corrected in some cases by those of New York. Eggs are reckoned as costing in the spring 18 cts., in Fall and Winter 25 cts., canned fruit is put down at the price paid for the fruit in Summer. The cost of raw material is given in all cases, bread being reckoned at the cost of the flour contained in it.

In three different seasons, four days in succession are selected, these days being the ones considered most trying to the housekeeper—Saturday, Sunday, Monday and Tuesday, and this gives an opportunity to show how the food should be planned and cooked ahead. It is intended that on Saturday the food for Sunday should be cooked as nearly as possible, as the Sunday dinner should be a good one but requiring a minimum of labor on that day; the dinner on Monday should be such as can be cooked on the back of the stove and in the oven.

The recipes will have to be varied a little according to advice given in appropriate places as to economy, *e. g.*, substituting beef fat for butter, or adding it when skim milk is used instead of whole milk.

It is intended that each day there shall be a small surplus of money for purchasing seasonings and flavors.

INTRODUCTION TO BILLS OF FARE, CLASS I.

(*To the Mother of the Family.*)

In the general introduction the writer has stated a

few principles that should guide us in choosing our food. We have learned that to keep us in good health and working order we ought to have a certain amount of what is best furnished by meat, eggs, milk and other animal products, and that we must also have fats as well as what is given us in grains and vegetables.

But now our work has only just begun for we are to furnish these food principles in the shape of cooked dishes to be put on the family table three times a day, and the dishes must not only be nourishing but they must taste good, and there must be plenty of variety from day to day; and last—and this is the hardest point of all—we are to try to do this for the sum of *13 cents per person daily.*

I am going to consider myself as talking to the mother of a family who has six mouths to feed, and no more money than this to do it with. Perhaps this woman has never kept accurate accounts and does not know whether she spends more or less than this sum. She very likely has her "flush" days and her "poor" days according to the varying amounts of the family earnings, and it may be a comfort to her to know that if she could average these days and plan a little better, she can feed her family nicely on this sum.

A few facts as to what the writer knows to have been done in this line will not be amiss. I knew a family of 6 belonging to one of the professional classes, half, grown people, and half, children, that lived for a year on an average of 11 cents per person daily, and no one would have said that they did not live well enough; they had meat about four days out of the seven, there was always cake on their supper table, and they used plenty of fruit.

Here is an average bill of fare. Breakfast — milk toast, fried potatoes, coffee; dinner — soup made of shank of beef, fried liver, rice and potatoes; supper — bread and butter fried mush, stewed pears and cake. Next day there was pressed beef made from the soup meat chopped and flavored, and next day there was cheap fish nicely fried. The head of this household was a skillful economist, absolutely no mistakes were made in cooking, and not a scrap was wasted, she had a long list of simple dishes at her command and she especially studied variety. "I abandon even a favorite dish for weeks," she said, "if any one tires of it." I give this as a sample of what I know to have been done by a highly respectable family in a city of small size in one of our eastern states.

It must be mentioned that the price on which this family lived in comfort could not have been as low as it was but for one great help; they had a small garden that furnished green vegetables and a little fruit. But then almost every family has some special advantage that would lower the rate somewhat; one buys butter or fruit advantageously of friends in the country, another can buy at wholesale when certain staples are cheapest, still another may be able to keep a few fowls, and so on. Numerous instances could be brought to prove that the food for a family can be purchased in a raw condition for the sum per head for which we have undertaken to buy it, and that by skill in cooking, flavoring and giving right variety, a healthful and very acceptable diet can be furnished, though it cannot, of course, contain luxuries.

Another thing, when I speak of a woman who is to buy the food of a family for 13 cents apiece daily, I have in mind the wife of a man who earns this sum himself, the wife having her time to attend to the housework and children. If a woman helps earn, as in a factory, doing most of her housework after she comes home at night, she must certainly have more money than in the first case in order to accomplish the same result, for she must buy her bread already baked and can only cook those dishes that take the least time.

I shall take for granted that you have the kitchen utensils described on page 20; if not, buy them, because, you cannot afford to do without them. Food is very expensive compared with pots and pans; you must not spoil food for lack of the right things to cook it in.

I only ask you in advance to try the recipes I shall give and to try to lay aside your prejudices against dishes to which you are not accustomed, as soups and cheese dishes for instance. You cannot afford to reject anything that will vary your diet, for many good tasting things you cannot buy.

I know it is hard for a busy woman to give to her cooking a bit more time than will "just do," but if you make it a rule to determine the night beforehand just what you will cook on the following day, no matter how simple the food may be, you will gain this result; with the materials at your disposal you will put before your family much better food, and they will call you a good cook and think that no family need live better than they; and this impression will be made principally from your having the right variety. Let us understand, to begin with, that it is your business in life just now to conquer this food question as it affects your family. Just as the business man must watch the market and take advantage of a half cent a pound on an article, that he may successfully compete with his neighbor, so you must be on the alert to use every possible advantage. It is a struggle in which energy and calculation will tell for a great deal, and you will have solid enjoyment in every point that you gain.

In buying meat your saving cannot be so much in quantity as in quality. Try to learn the different parts of an animal, and to distinguish between meat from a fat ox and that from a lean one, for, as we have explained, the former has less water in it, and why should you pay good money for that which nature gives you free? In winter, try to buy meat ahead so that you can make it tender by keeping it, and you will notice, too, that the larger the piece you buy the smaller is the per cent of bone you get with it. The per cent of bone in the whole animal, as in the case of an ox, is not more than 10 or 11 per cent, but the buyer of a small piece of meat often gets twice that proportion. As we have said again and again in these pages, the low-priced or tougher parts have as much nutriment for you as the rib roast which is beyond your purse. Choose often the fat middle rib and cook it long and slowly; buy the neck and scrag of mutton, and make a stew with vegetables; buy half a calf's head, and see what a fine soup you can make of it. Have beef's liver now and then, and tripe, rather than put your money into sausage of doubtful quality. By all means buy fish when it is cheap, catfish, for instance, which are excellent fried. Keep suet always on hand and use instead of butter, as has been directed.

No one need tell you how valuable salt pork and bacon are for you,—the only danger is that you will use too much of them.

In buying eggs, you must be governed by the price; in winter use as few as possible, and even in the spring when they are cheapest, remember that they are not as cheap as the lowest priced cuts of meat from fat animals. But when they cost only 15 cents a dozen you can well disregard any small comparison of nutritive values, in consideration of their high worth in furnishing variety; you can afford to use them now and then in the place of meat and in making the various egg dishes.

Of the value of cheese as a regular dish to take the place of meat, you can read in another part of this essay. Buy it once a week at least, the skim variety, if you cannot afford the others, and grate or cook it according to the recipes given.

Try to find a reliable milkman and buy skim milk at half the price of full, and use it for all cooking purposes, keeping full milk, and, if possible, a little of the cream, for coffee.

Now let us take the vegetable part of your diet.

Grains.

You must keep on hand every kind of flour and grain that is not too expensive; be thankful that wheat flour is so good and so cheap, it will be your best friend. If you are not already skillful in using it in bread and other doughs, you will waste your materials and make mistakes at first, but there is nothing for you but to become mistress of this department of cookery. Use bread freely in all the bread dishes, learn how to make every one. You will use buckwheat for cakes, rice for puddings, barley in soups, oatmeal and cornmeal for mushes, and you must learn to use them all in as many ways as possible. The grains are cheaper foods for us than vegetables, although dried peas, beans and lentils follow hard upon them. Even the potato, which may be called our favorite vegetable, is more expensive than wheat flour, if we are talking only of food values.

Except in the height of their season, have nothing to do with green vegetables, at least not under the impression that they are cheap; if you buy them, know that you are paying for flavors and variety, rather than for food. But even in the early spring, buy plenty of such vegetables as onions, carrots, parsley and other green herbs for your soups and stews. When you go for a walk in the country, be sure to bring home mint and sorrel in your pocket; the former will make you a nice meat sauce, the latter a delightful flavor in soup. It will be perfectly easy for you to grow in a window box that delicious herb, parsley, and have it always fresh.

For a low purse, there is no help so great as a knowledge of flavorings. When we remember that we can live on bread, beans, peas and a little cheap meat and fat the year round if we can only make it "go down," we shall realize the importance of such additions as rouse the appetite; there is room here for all your skill and all your invention. Always make a cheap but nutritious dish inviting in appearance; especially does this influence the appetites of children who are delighted with a very plain cake if only a few raisins or some sugar appear on the top.

The Bills of Fare on pages 146 to 158, where 78 cents covers the cost of food for a family of 6 per day, and where the amount of food is carefully weighed and estimated, is meant only to suggest to you how in a few cases your food problem can be solved. You can, no doubt, spend the money in ways that will better suit the tastes of your family, but I beg you to examine anew your favorite dishes to see if they are as nutritious as they should be for their price. Remember that the Proteid column is the one that you must look to most carefully because it is furnished at the most expense, and it is very important that it should not fall below the figures I have given. If, for instance, you should economize in meat in order to buy cake and pastry, this column would suffer at the expense of the other two and your family would be under nourished.

BILLS OF FARE, CLASS I.

For family of six, average price 78 cents per day, or 13 cents per person.

SATURDAY, MAY.

Breakfast.

Flour Pancakes,
(p. 103) with Sugar Syrup.
Coffee.

Dinner.

Bread Soup (p. 20).
Beefneck Stew
Noodles (p. 90).
Swelled Rice Pudding (p. 107).

Supper.

Browned Flour Soup, with Fried Bread (p. 121).
Toast and Cheese (page 62, No. 1).

	Proteids. oz.	Fats. oz.	Carbo-hydrates. oz.	Cost in Cents.
½ lb. Rice	.64	.08	6.12	4
1 lb. Sugar	....	....	15.42	7
¾ lb. Fat Cheese	3.00	3.48	.24	11¼
2 qts. Skim Milk	2.12	.48	3.30	8
2 lb. Flour	3.84	.48	22.88	6
½ qt. Whole Milk	.58	.62	.83	3½
2 Eggs	.34	.32	....	3
2½ lbs. Beef neck	8.40	2.20	....	20
⅜ lb. Suet	....	5.88	....	3
⅛ lb. Coffee	....	....	....	3⅜
3½ lbs. Bread	3.36	.28	29.06	8 1/10
Total	22.28	13.82	77.85	77⅛
Required	19.19	12.42	78.08	78

SUNDAY, MAY.

Breakfast.
Milk Toast.
Coffee.

Dinner.
Stuffed Beef's Heart (p. 48).
Potatoes stewed with Milk.
Dried Apple Pie (p. 108).
Bread and Cheese.
Corn Coffee (p. 135).

Supper.
Noodle Soup (from Saturday, p. 91).
Broiled Herring.
Bread.
Tea.

	Proteids. oz.	Fats. oz.	Carbo-hydrates. oz.	Cost in Cents.
Heart of Fat Ox weighing 2 lbs.	5.76	2.56	....	10
4 lbs. Bread	3.84	.32	33.22	9⅛
¾ lb. Sugar	....	....	11.88	5
1 qt. Skim Milk	1.06	.24	1.65	4
½ lb. Dried Apples	.10	....	4.50	6
1½ lb. Flour	2.88	.36	17.16	4½
12 Smoked Herring (1 pound).	3.36	1.36	....	10
¼ lb. Suet	....	9.23	....	2
2 lbs. Potatoes	.64	....	6.62	2½
¼ lb. Butter	....	3.33	....	6¼
½ lb. Skim Cheese	2.40	1.07	40	4
Tea	....	....	....	2
⅛ lb. Coffee	....	....	....	3⅗
1 qt. Whole Milk	1.16	1.23	1.65	7
Total	21.20	14.39	77.08	76
Required	19.19	12.42	78.03	78

MONDAY, MAY.

Breakfast.
Oatmeal Mush, with
Milk and Sugar.
Bread.
Coffee.

Dinner.
Pea Soup (p. 117).
Mutton Stew (p. 52).
Boiled Potatoes.
Bread.

Supper.

Bread Pancakes (p. 93).
Fried Bacon.
Tea.

	Proteids. oz.	**Fats.** oz.	Carbo-hydrates. oz.	Cost in Cents.
2 Eggs	.34	.32	....	3
¾ lb. Oatmeal	1.74	.72	7.80	3¾
⅛ lb. Coffee	....	....	....	3⅝
½ lb. Sugar	....	....	7.92	3⅓
1½ qts. Skim Milk	1.59	.36	1.48	6
¾ lb. Bacon	.36	9.60	....	9
4 lbs. Potatoes	1.28	....	13.24	5
4 lbs. Bread	3.84	**.32**	31.20	9⅕
1 qt. Whole Milk	1.16	**1.24**	1.66	7
3 lbs. Shoulder of Mutton	8.16	**2.88**	....	21
1 lb. Peas, Dried	3.68	**.32**	8.32	5
½ lb. Flour	**.06**	**.12**	5.72	1⅓
Total	23.11	**15.88**	80.34	77.3
Required	19.10	**12.42**	78.03	78

TUESDAY, MAY.

Breakfast.

Oatmeal Mush and Milk.
Buttered Toast.
Coffee.

Dinner.

Fried Catfish
with Mint Sauce (p. 73).
Fried Potatoes.
Bread.

Supper.

Fried Farina Pudding (p. 107).
Broiled Salt Pork.
Bread.
Tea.

	Proteids. oz.	Fats. oz.	Carbo-hydrates. oz.	Cost in Cents.
1 lb. Oatmeal	2.32	.96	10.40	5
1 qt. Whole Milk	1.16	1.23	1.65	7
1 qt. Skim Milk	1.06	.24	1.65	4
$3\frac{1}{2}$ lbs. Catfish	7.00	.20	....	$17\frac{1}{2}$
$1\frac{1}{2}$ lbs. Farina	2.50	...	18.22	$7\frac{1}{2}$
2 eggs	.34	.32	....	3
$4\frac{1}{2}$ lbs. Bread	4.32	.36	37.36	$10\frac{35}{100}$
Coffee	....	....	....	$3\frac{3}{8}$
2 lbs. Potatoes	.64	....	6.62	$2\frac{1}{2}$
$\frac{5}{8}$ lb. Salt Pork	.30	8.00	....	$7\frac{1}{2}$
$\frac{1}{8}$ lb. Butter	....	1.67	....	$3\frac{1}{8}$
$\frac{1}{4}$ lb. Sugar	....	....	3.96	$1\frac{3}{4}$
Tea	....	....	....	2
Total	19.64	12.98	79.86	$74\frac{3}{5}$
Required	19.19	12.42	78.03	78

SATURDAY, SEPTEMBER.

Breakfast.

Soda Biscuit.
Baked Potatoes with
Drawn Butter Sauce.
Cocoa.

Dinner.

Pea Soup (p. 117)
Irish Stew.
Bread.

Supper.

Corn Mush and Molasses.
Bread and Grated Cheese.
Tea.

	Proteids. oz.	**Fats.** oz.	Carbo-hydrates. oz.	Cost in Cents.
1 lb. Dried Peas	**3.68**	.32	8.32	5
2 lbs. Scrag of Mutton	**5.44**	1.92	....	16
3 lbs. Potatoes	.96	....	9.94	3¾
3 lbs. Bread	2.88	.24	24.90	6 9/10
2 lbs. Cornmeal	3.14	.90	19.50	6
¼ lb. Sugar	....	....	3.96	1¼
¼ lb. Fat Cheese	**1.00**	1.56	.08	3¾
1 qt. Whole Milk	**1.16**	1.23	1.65	7
¼ lb. Butter	....	3.33	....	6 3/10
1½ lbs. Flour	2.88	**.36**	17.16	6¾
¼ lb. Suet	....	**3.92**	....	2
¼ lb. Molasses	....	....	2.48	2⅛
Cocoa Shells	....	....	....	2
Tea	....	....	....	2
Total	21.14	13.78	87.99	71⅛
Required	19.19	12.42	78.03	78

SUNDAY, **SEPTEMBER.**

Breakfast.

Oatmeal and Milk.
Bread and Butter.
Cocoa.

Dinner.

Broiled Beef's Liver.
Boiled Potatoes and Carrots with Fried Onions (p. 116).
Bread and Cheese.

Supper.

Lentil Soup with Fried Bread (p. 118).
Smoked Herring.
Bread. Barley Porridge (p. 122).

	Proteids. oz.	Fats. oz.	Carbo-hydrates. oz.	Cost in Cents.
1¼ lbs. Beef's Liver	4.80	.96	....	15
3 lbs. Potatoes	.96	....	9.94	3¾
1 lb. Carrots	....	....	1.44	1½
1½ lbs. Oatmeal	3.48	1.44	15.60	7½
½ lb. Lentils	2.04	.16	4.32	5
1½ qt. Whole Milk	1.74	1.85	2.48	10½
½ lb. Sugar	....	....	7.92	3½
¼ lb. Pearl Barley	.44	.06	2.86	2
¼ lb. Suet	....	3.92	....	2
4 lbs. Bread	3.84	.32	33.20	$9\frac{1}{5}$
6 Smoked Herring (8 oz.)	1.68	.68	....	5
¼ lb. Butter	....	3.33	....	6¼
¼ lb. Fat Cheese	1.00	1.16	....	3¾
Cocoa Shells	....	....	....	2
Total	19.98	13.88	77.76	$76\frac{9}{10}$
Required	19.19	12.42	78.03	78

MONDAY, SEPTEMBER.

Breakfast.

Buckwheat Cakes.
Fried Bacon.
Coffee.

Dinner.

Giblet Soup (p. 58).
Baked Potatoes with
Drawn Butter Sauce.
Bread.

Supper.

Codfish Balls (p. 57).
Cheese.
Bread. Tea.

	Proteids. oz.	Fats. oz.	Carbo-hydrates. oz.	Cost in Cents.
2 lbs. Buckwheat Flour	3.04	.64	23.30	10
Giblets	2.20	.12	....	8
3 lbs. Potatoes	.96	....	9.94	3¾
¾ lb. Bacon	.36	9.60	....	9
4½ lbs. Bread	4.32	.36	37.36	$10\frac{15}{100}$
½ lb. Sugar	....	....	7.92	3½
¾ lb. Fat Cheese	3.	2.48	.24	11¼
1 lb. Salt Codfish	4.80	.16	....	8
Tea	....	....	....	2
1 qt. Whole Milk	1.16	1.23	1.65	7
⅛ lb. Coffee	....	....	....	3⅜
Total	19.84	15.59	80.41	76¾
Required	19.19	12.42	78.03	78

TUESDAY, SEPTEMBER.

Breakfast.

Fried Bacon.
Boiled Potatoes.
Bread. Coffee.

Dinner.

Boiled Corned Beef
with Horseradish Sauce.
Stewed Cabbage.
Bread.
Barley Porridge (p. 122).

Supper.

Pea Soup.
Yeast Biscuit and Butter.
Stewed Fruit.

	Proteids. oz.	Fats. oz.	Carbo-hydrates. oz.	Cost in Cents.
1½ lbs. Corn Beef	6.96	1.54	....	15
3 lbs. Cabbage	.80	....	2.	6
2 lbs. Flour	3.84	.48	22.88	6
2 lbs. Potatoes	.64	....	6.62	2½
1 lb. Dried Peas	3.68	.32	8.32	5
3½ lbs. Bread	3.36	.28	29.06	$8\frac{1}{16}$
½ lb. Bacon	.24	6.40	....	6
¼ lb. Butter	....	3.38	....	6¼
⅛ lb. Suet	....	1.96	....	1
½ lb. Pearl Barley	.88	.12	5.72	4
1 qt. Skim Milk	1.06	.24	1.65	4
1 pt. Whole Milk	.58	.62	.83	3½
⅛ lb. Coffee	....	....	....	$3\frac{4}{10}$
½ lb. Sugar	....	....	7.92	3½
Fruit	....	....	....	3
Total	22.04	15.29	85.	$77\frac{1}{8}$
Required	19.19	12.42	78.03	78

SATURDAY, JANUARY.

Breakfast.

Fried Bacon.
Corn Bread (p. 103).
Coffee.

Dinner.

Browned Flour Soup (p. 121).
Stewed Mutton.
Mashed Potatoes.
Bread.

Supper.

Baked Beans. Bread.
Apple Dumplings (p. 108),
with Pudding Sauce (p. 112).
Tea.

	Proteids. oz.	Fats. oz.	Carbo-hydrates. oz.	Cost in Cents.
3 lbs. Neck of Mutton	8.16	2.88	....	24
3 lbs. Potatoes	.08	....	9.94	3¾
4 lbs. Bread	3.84	.32	33.20	9½
1 lb. Flour	1.92	.24	11.44	3
2 lbs. Corn Meal	3.14	1.20	22.40	6
1 lb. Beans	3.68	.32	8.56	5
½ lb. Sugar	....	....	7.92	3¼
½ lb. Bacon	.24	6.44	....	6
¼ lb. Suet	....	1.96	....	1
⅙ lb. Coffee	....	....	....	3⅖
1 qt. Whole Milk	1.16	1.23	1.65	7
Apples	....	....	....	2
Tea	....	....	....	2
Total	23.10	14.59	95.11	75⅕
Required	19.19	12.42	78.63	78

SUNDAY, JANUARY.

Breakfast.

Fried Codfish.
Bread and Butter.
Coffee.

Dinner.

Sheep's Head Stew
with Soda Biscuit Dumplings.
Baked Potatoes.
Bread and Grated Cheese.
Cocoa.

Supper.

Potato and Onion Salad.
Broiled Salt Pork. Bread.
Corn Mush with Pudding Sauce (p. 112).

	Proteids. oz.	Fats. oz.	Carbo-hydrates. oz.	Cost in Cents.
2 lbs. Corn Meal	3.14	1.20	22.40	6
1 qt. Skim Milk	1.06	.24	1.65	4
1 pt. Whole Milk	.58	.62	.83	3½
½ lb. Sugar	....	....	7.92	3½
3 lbs. Bread	2.88	.24	24.90	6 $\frac{9}{10}$
1 lb. Salt Codfish	4.80	....	....	8
½ lb. Butter	....	6.66	....	12½
¼ lb. Skim Cheese	1.20	.53	.20	2
4 lbs. Potatoes	1.28	....	13.25	5
¼ lb. Salt Pork	.12	3.20	....	3
¼ lb. Suet	....	3.92	....	2
¾ lb. Flour	1.44	.18	8.58	2¼
1 Sheep's Head, assumed to contain 1½ lbs. meat	4.08	1.44	....	12
Onions	....	....	....	2
Cocoa Shells	....	....	....	2
Coffee	....	....	....	3$\frac{2}{5}$
Total	20.58	18,23	79.73	78
Required	19.19	12.42	78,08	78

MONDAY, JANUARY.

Breakfast.

Fried Mush and Molasses.
Bread.
Coffee.

Dinner.

Soup (from Boiled Beef)
with Macaroni.
Boiled Beef Flank
with Mustard Sauce.
Bean Puree.
Bread.

Supper.

Boiled Potatoes with
Butter Gravy.
Dried Apple Roly Poly Pudding (p. 108).
Bread. Tea.

	Proteids oz.	Fats oz.	Carbo-hydrates oz.	Cost in Cents
2 lb. Beef Flank	6.72	1.76	....	16
1 lb. Beans	3.68	.32	8.56	5
½ lb. Dried Apples	.10	....	4.50	6
2 lbs. Potatoes	.64	....	6.02	2¼
2 lbs. Corn Meal	3.14	1.20	22.40	6
1½ lbs. Flour	2.88	.36	17.16	4½
¼ lb. Butter	....	3.33	....	6¼
¼ lb. Suet	....	3.92	....	2
¼ lb. Molasses	....	....	2.48	2½
½ lb. Sugar	....	....	7.92	3½
3 lbs. bread	2.88	.24	24.90	6 2/10
1 qt. Whole Milk	1.16	1.23	1.65	7
⅛ lb. Coffee	....	....	....	3⅜
Tea	....	....	....	2
¼ lb. Macaroni	.30	.02	3.06	3¼
Total	21.50	12.38	99.25	77 1/10
Required	19.19	12.42	78.03	78

Tuesday, January.

Breakfast.

Fried Potatoes.
Bread.
Coffee.

Dinner.

Browned Farina Soup with Toast (p. 121).
Stewed Mutton, with Yeast Dumplings.

Supper.

Bean Soup.
Milk Toast.
Tea.

	Proteids oz.	Fats oz.	Carbo-hydrates oz.	Cost in Cents
2½ lbs. Mutton	6.80	2.40	....	20
1 qt. Skim Milk	1.06	.24	1.65	4
1½ lbs. Beans	5.52	.48	12.84	7½
¼ lb. Butter	....	3.33	....	6¼
½ lb. Suet	....	7.84	....	4
½ lb. Sugar	....	....	7.92	3½
3 lbs. Potatoes	.96	....	9.94	4¼
1½ lbs. Flour	2.88	.36	17.16	4½
1 qt. Whole Milk	1.16	1.23	1.65	7
3 lbs. Bread	2.88	.24	24.90	$6\frac{9}{10}$
¼ lb. Farina	.42	....	3.03	1¾
⅛ lb Coffee	....	....	....	$3\frac{2}{5}$
Tea	....	....	....	
Total	21.68	16.12	79.09	75
Required	19.19	12.42	78.03	78

BILLS OF FARE, CLASS II.

For family of six. Average price $1.26 per day, or 18 cts. per person.

The bills of fare in this class will not be given in detail. Taking those given for Class I as a basis, it is expected that certain luxuries will be added and a better quality of food used; the quantities of Proteid, Fat and Carbohydrate will then not be lowered, which is the point of greatest importance.

BILLS OF FARE, CLASS III.

For family of six. Average price, $1.38 per day, or 23 cents per person.

SATURDAY, MAY.

Breakfast.

Oranges.
Egg Omelet on Toast.
Boiled Rice with Milk and Sugar.
Coffee.

Dinner.

Beef Soup with Egg Sponge (p. 128).
Macaroni with Cheese (p. 90).
Dandelion Greens.
Bread.

Supper.

Sour Cream Soup (p. 124).
Meat Croquettes (of soup meat) (p. 49).
Graham Bread and Butter.
Tea. Cake.

	Proteids oz.	Fats oz.	Carbo-hydrates oz.	Cost in Cents
1 lb. Rice	1.28	.16	12.24	8
½ lb. Sugar	....	....	7.92	3½
6 Oranges	....	....	....	10
¾ lb. Macaroni	1.08	....	9.18	12¾
4 lbs. Bread	3.84	.32	33.22	9⅕
2 lbs. Flour	3.84	.48	22.88	6
⅛ lb. Coffee	....	....	....	3⅜
2 qts. Whole Milk	2.32	2.46	3.30	14
10 Eggs	1.70	1.60	....	15
2½ lbs. Meat	8.40	2.20	....	20
¾ lb. Butter	....	9.90	....	18¾
½ lb. Fat Cheese	2.00	2.32	.16	7½
Sour Cream and flavors for soup	....	....	....	6
Tea	....	....	....	2
Total	24.46	19.53	88.90	136 1/10
Required	19.19	12.42	78.03	138

Sunday, May.

Breakfast.

Oatmeal Mush with sugar and milk.
Bread and Butter.
Coffee.

Dinner.

Ham and Eggs.
Salad of Cold Beans and Lettuce
Rhubarb Pie.
Cocoa.
Bread.

Supper.

Rice Pancakes (p. 93), with Sugar Syrup.
Stewed Potatoes.
Tea.

	Proteids oz.	Fats oz.	Carbo-hydrates oz.	Cost in Cents.
¾ lb. Oatmeal	1.74	0.72	7.80	3⅓
⅛ lb. Coffee	....	....	....	3⅓
1 lb. Sugar	....	....	15.84	7
2 qts. Whole Milk	2.32	2.46	3.30	14
¾ lb. Butter	....	9.99	....	18¾
1 lb. Ham	3.84	5.84	....	25
⅛ lb. Suet	....	1.96	....	1
12 Eggs	2.04	1.92	....	18
Cocoa	....	....	....	4
3 lbs. Potatoes	.96	....	9.94	3¾
4 lbs. Bread	3.84	.32	33.20	9½
⅛ lb. Lettuce	.10	....	.20	5
1 lb. Beans	3.68	.32	8.55	5
Rhubarb	....	....	....	4
½ lb. Rice	.64	.08	6.12	4
1¼ lbs. Flour	2.88	.36	17.16	4⅛
Tea	....	....	....	2
Salad Dressing	....	....	....	5
Total	22.04	23.97	102.11	137
Required	19.19	12.42	78.03	138

MONDAY, MAY.

Breakfast.

Oranges.
Milk Toast.
Coffee.

Dinner.

Roast Mutton and Bread Dressing (p. 106).
Mashed Potatoes.
Corn Mush with Sugar and Milk.
Soda Cream (p. 136).

Supper.

Parsnip Soup (p. 119), with Yeast Dumplings (p. 128).
Bread and butter.
Sponge Cake. Tea.

	Proteids oz.	Fats oz.	Carbo-hydrates oz.	Cost in Cents
3½ lbs. Bread	3.36	.28	29.06	$8\frac{1}{15}$
3 lbs. Mutton	8.16	2.88	....	48
2 qts. Whole Milk	2.32	2.46	3.30	14
1½ lbs. Sugar	....	....	23.76	10½
1 lb. Flour	1.92	.24	11.44	3
½ lb. Butter	....	6.66	....	13½
⅛ lb. Coffee	....	....	....	3⅗
6 Oranges	....	....	....	10
2 lb. Cornmeal	3.14	1.20	22.40	6
4 Eggs	.68	.64	....	6
3 lbs. Potatoes	.96	....	9.94	3¾
Tea	....	....	....	2
Soda Cream	....	....	....	3
Parsnips	....	....	....	6
Total	20.54	14.36	99.90	136¼
Required	19.19	12.42	78.03	138

Tuesday, May.

Breakfast.

Buttered Toast.
Coffee.
Canned Fruit.

Dinner.

Sorrel Soup (p. 120.)
Fried Catfish.
Noodles (p. 90.)
Bread.
Swelled Rice Pudding (p. 107).

Supper.

Fried Mush.
Stewed Rhubarb.
Fresh Rusks and Butter (p. 98).
Tea.

	Proteids. oz.	Fats. oz.	Carbo-hydrates. oz.	Cost in Cents.
Canned Fruit	....	....	....	15
2 lbs. Corn Meal	3.14	1.20	22.40	6
3 lbs. Bread	2.88	.24	24.90	6 9/10
1½ qts. Whole Milk	1.74	1.86	2.50	10½
2 qts. Skim Milk	2.12	.48	3.30	8
Rhubarb	....	....	....	8
2 lbs. Flour	3.84	.48	22.88	6
1 lb. Butter	....	13.33	....	25
½ lb. Sugar	....	....	7.92	3½
Sorrel &c. for Soup	....	....	....	5
½ lb. Rice	.64	.08	6.12	4
¼ lb. Suet	....	3.92	....	2
3 lbs. Fresh Fish	8.00	.24	....	18
½ lb. Coffee	....	....	....	3⅜
4 Eggs	.08	.64	....	6
Tea	....	....	....	2
Total	23.04	22.47	90.02	120 8/10
Required	19.19	12.42	78.08	188

Saturday, September.

Breakfast.

Hominy Mush with
Sugar Syrup
Stewed Pears.
Toasted Crackers.
Coffee.

Dinner.

Plum Soup (p. 125).
Broiled Beef Steak.
Boiled Green Corn.
Turnips and Potatoes (p. 116).
Bread.
Apple Pie (p. 109).

Supper.

Irish Stew (p. 52).
Biscuit and Butter.
Yeast Doughnuts (p. 99).
Tea.

	Proteids. oz.	Fats. oz.	Carbo-hydrates. oz.	Cost in Cents.
1 lb. Hominy	1.58	.60	11.20	5
Pears and Plums	....	....	....	5
2 lbs. Bread	1.92	.16	16.60	4 3/5
1/8 lb. Crackers	.50	....	4.15	5
2 lbs. Beef Steak	6.72	1.76	....	36
1 doz. Green Corn	....	....	....	15
2 lbs. Potatoes	.64	....	6.62	2 1/2
Apples	....	....	....	4
1 lb. Turnips	.15	....	1.12	0 7/10
3 lbs. Flour	5.76	.64	34.32	9
1/8 lb. Suet	....	1.96	....	1
1 lb. Mutton	2.72	.96	....	8
3/4 lb. Butter	....	9.99	....	18 3/4
2 Eggs	.34	.32	....	4 1/5
Tea	....	....	....	2
1 lb. Sugar	....	....	15.84	7
1 qt. Whole Milk	1.16	1.23	1.65	7
1/8 lb. Coffee	....	....	....	3 3/5
Total	20.83	17.62	91.50	138 1/10
Required	10.19	12.42	78.03	138

SUNDAY, SEPTEMBER.

Breakfast.

Sour Milk Pancakes with
Sugar Syrup (p. 103).
Sausage. Bread.
Cucumbers.
Coffee.

Dinner.

Green Corn Soup (p. 120).
Fricaseed Chicken (p. 57).
Potatoes and Carrots (p. 116).
with Fried Onions.
Bread.

Supper.

Fried Farina Pudding (p. 108.
Water Toast.
Radishes.
Tea.

	Proteids. oz.	Fats. oz.	Carbo-hydrates. oz.	Cost in Cents.
Radishes	....	....	....	3
1 lb. Sausage	2.32	6.00	....	12
¾ lb. Sugar	....	....	9.00	6¾
1½ qts. Whole Milk	1.74	1.85	2.48	10½
3 lbs. Bread	2.88	.24	24.90	6 3/10
½ doz. Green Corn	....	....	....	7½
An Old Chicken (3 lbs.)	9.00	1.00	....	50
2 lbs. Potatoes	.60	....	6.60	2½
½ lb. Carrots	....	....	.72	1
Cucumbers	....	....	....	2
1½ lb. Flour	2.88	.36	17.16	4½
½ lb. Farina	.84	....	6.00	2½
¼ lb. Butter	....	3.38	....	6¼
1 qt. Sour Milk	1.06	.24	1.65	4
Coffee	....	....	....	3¾
Tea	....	....	....	2
2 Eggs	.34	.32	....	4½
Total	21.66	14.24	60.41	127½
Required	19.19	12.42	78.08	138

MONDAY, SEPTEMBER.

Breakfast.

Codfish Balls.
Bread and Butter.
Coffee.
Stewed Apples.

Dinner.

Roast Beef.
Baked Potatoes.
Stewed Tomatoes.
Lemonade.
Bread.

Supper.

Berry Roly Poly (p. 108).
Cheese.
Bread and Butter.
Tea.

	Proteids. oz.	Fats. oz.	Carbo-hydrates. oz.	Cost in Cents.
¾ lb. Codfish	3.60	....	....	6
4 lbs. Potatoes	1.28	....	13.24	5
3 lbs. Bread	2.88	.24	24.90	6 3/10
¾ lb. Butter	....	9.99	....	18¾
2 qts. Whole Milk	2.32	2.46	3.30	14
1 lb. Sugar	....	....	15.84	7
2½ lbs. Beef	8.40	2.20	....	40
3 lbs. Tomatoes	....	....	4.00	5
Lemons	....	....	....	7
1⅛ lb. Flour	3.88	.36	17.16	4½
½ lb. Fat Cheese	2.00	2.32	.18	7½
⅛ lb. Coffee	....	....	....	3⅗
Tea	....	....	....	2
Fruit	....	....	....	10
Total	24.36	17.57	78.62	137
Required	19.19	12.42	78.03	138

TUESDAY, SEPTEMBER.

Breakfast.

Broiled Mackerel.
Stewed Potatoes.
Bread and Butter.
Coffee.

Dinner.

Sour Cream Soup (p. 124).
Roast Mutton
with Bread Stuffing.
Boiled Beets.
Bread Pudding (p. 111, No. 2).

Supper.

Apple Fritters (p. 114),
with Sugar Syrup.
Bread and Butter.
Tea.

	Proteids. oz.	Fats. oz.	Carbo-hydrates. oz.	Cost in Cents.
1½ lbs. Flour	2.88	.36	17.16	4½
4 Eggs	.68	.64	....	8⅓
2 qts. Whole Milk	2.32	2.46	3.30	14
1 lb. Sugar	....	....	15.84	7
⅛ lb. Suet	....	1.96	....	1
2½ lbs. Mutton	6.80	2.40	....	40
2 lbs. Beets	....	....	3.00	5
1½ lbs. Salt Mackerel	4.56	3.00	....	18¾
1½ lbs. Potatoes	.48	....	4.96	1 2/5
4 lbs. Bread	3.84	.32	33.20	9⅗
½ lb. Butter	....	6.66	....	12½
Sour Cream and Apples	....	....	....	8
⅛ lb. Coffee	....	....	....	3¾
Tea	....	....	....	2
Total	21.56	17.80	79.46	135½
Required	19.19	12.42	78.03	138

Saturday, January.

Breakfast.

Buckwheat Cakes and Sugar Syrup.
Bread and Butter.
Coffee.

Dinner.

Roast Fresh Pork, with Apple Sauce.
Mashed Potatoes.
Indian Pudding (p. 110).
Bread.

Supper.

Herring and Potato Salad.
Lentils, with Prunes (p. 116).
Bread and Butter.
Tea.

	Proteids. oz.	Fats. oz.	Carbo-hydrates. oz.	Cost in Cents.
2 lbs. Buckwheat Flour	3.04	.64	23.20	10
1½ lbs. Corn Meal	2.28	.91	16.80	4½
1 lb. Butter	....	13.33	....	25
¾ lb. Sugar	....	....	11.88	5¼
1 qt. Whole Milk	1.16	1.23	1.65	7
Apples	....	....	....	4
2½ lbs. Fresh Pork	8.00	2.80	....	37½
3 lbs. Potatoes	.96	....	9.94	3⅓
2 Eggs	.34	.32	....	4⅙
1 qt. Skim Milk	1.16	.24	1.65	4
3 lbs. Bread	2.88	.24	24.90	6 9/10
½ lb. Lentils	2.04	.16	4.32	5
½ lb. Prunes	.15	....	3.80	5
⅛ lb. Coffee	....	....	....	3⅜
Tea	....	....	....	2
6 Herrings	1.68	.68	....	5
Salad Dressing	....	....	....	5
Total	23.69	20.55	98.14	137½
Required	19.19	12.42	78.03	138

SUNDAY, JANUARY.

Breakfast.
Milk Toast.
Fried Potatoes.
Coffee.

Dinner.
Cold Roast Pork,
Noodles (p. 90).
Stewed Cabbage.
Bread.
Swelled Rice Pudding (p. 107).
Corn Coffee (p. 135).

Supper.

Potato Soup (p. 118). Grated Cheese.
Bread and butter.
Raised Cake (p. 98). Canned Fruit.
Tea.

	Proteids oz.	Fats oz.	Carbo-hydrates. oz.	Cost in Cents
¼ lb. Fat Cheese	1.08	.95	.06	3¾
4 lbs. Potatoes	1.28	....	13.24	5
2 lbs. Flour	3.84	48	22.88	6
4 Eggs	.68	.64	....	8½
2 qts. Whole Milk	2.32	2.46	3.30	14
1 qt. Skim Milk	1.06	.24	1.65	4
¾ lb. Butter	....	9.99	....	18¾
1 lb. Sugar	....	....	15.42	7
2 lbs. Fresh Pork	6.40	2.24	....	30
2 lbs. Cabbage	.80	....	1.60	8
⅙ lb. Rice	.64	.08	6.12	4
3 lbs. Bread	2.88	.24	24.90	6 9/10
Corn (dry grain)	....	....	....	2
Canned Fruit	....	....	....	10
⅙ lb. Coffee	....	....	....	3⅗
Tea	....	....	....	2
Total	20.98	17.32	89.17	133 1/10
Required	19.19	12.42	78.03	138

Monday, January.

Breakfast.

Buckwheat Cakes.
Sausage.
Coffee.
Apple Sauce.

Dinner.

Pea Soup (p. 118).
Roast Beef.
Baked Potatoes.
Canned Tomatoes.
Barley Gruel (p. 121).

Supper.

Potato Soup with Egg and Bread Balls (p. 128).
Brown Bread and Butter.
Canned Fruit. Tea.

	Proteids oz.	Fats oz.	Carbo-hydrates. oz.	Cost in Cents
2 lbs. Buckwheat Flour	3.04	.64	23.20	10
1 lb. Sausage	2.32	6.00	....	12
2 lbs. Beef	6.72	1.76	....	32
3 lbs. Potatoes	.96	....	9.94	$3\frac{3}{4}$
2 lbs. Tomatoes (canned at home)	.19	....	3.50	6
3 lbs. Bread	2.88	.24	24.90	$6\frac{9}{10}$
2 Eggs	.34	.32	....	$4\frac{1}{6}$
½ lb. Barley	.88	.12	5.72	4
1 qt. Whole Milk	1.16	1.23	1.65	7
½ lb. Sugar	....	....	7.92	$3\frac{1}{2}$
1 lb. Dried Peas	3.68	.32	8.32	5
½ lb. Butter	....	6.66	....	$12\frac{1}{2}$
Canned Fruit	....	....	....	10
⅛ lb. Coffee	....	....	....	$3\frac{3}{8}$
Tea	....	....	....	2
Apples	....	....	....	5
Total	22.17	17.29	85.15	$127\frac{1}{5}$
Required	19.19	12.42	78.03	138

TUESDAY, **JANUARY.**

Breakfast.

Graham Biscuits.
Fried Bacon. Apple Sauce.
Coffee.

Dinner.

Boiled **Mutton.**
Baked Potatoes.
Winter Squash.
Dried Apple Short Cake
with Pudding Sauce.
Corn Coffee.

Supper.

Mutton and Bean Broth.
Bread and Butter.
Cheese. Tea.
Cookies.

	Proteids oz.	Fats oz.	Carbo-hydrates oz.	Costs in Cent
¾ lb. Bacon	.36	9.66	....	9
½ lb. dried Apples	.10	....	4.44	6
1 lb. Beans	3.68	.32	8.56	5
¼ lb. Fat Cheese	1.00	1.16	....	3¾
1 lb. Sugar	....	....	15.84	7
2 qts. Whole Milk	2.22	2.46	3.30	14
2½ lbs. Mutton	6.80	2.40	....	30
3 lb. Potatoes	.96	....	9.94	3¾
2 lbs. Winter Squash	.16	....	3.20	10
Cookies	....	....	....	15
2 lbs. Bread	1.92	.16	16.60	4⅘
2½ lbs. Flour	4.80	.60	27.94	8½
½ lb. Butter	....	3.33	....	6¼
⅛ lb. Coffee	....	....	....	3⅘
Tea	....	....	....	2
Apples	....	....	....	5
Total	22.10	20.09	89.82	132 7/10
Required	19.19	12.42	78.08	138

TWELVE COLD DINNERS.

If a man is to eat a cold dinner for months or even for weeks, it is quite worth while to make that dinner as good as it can be, and to pack it nicely for carrying Every one knows how it can take the edge off even a keen appetite to find his sandwich smeared with apple pie, or his cake soaked with vinegar from the pickles. That a box or basket of given dimensions should hold as much as possible, and keep the different kinds of food separate, it must be divided into compartments.

Simplest—an oblong basket,—divide into two compartments by a piece of pasteboard cut so that it slips in rather tightly, then line the two compartments with nice wrapping paper put in fresh every day. It may be divided into four parts in the same way. A close fitting tin spice box is nice for holding cheese. A tiny "salve" box should contain salt and pepper mixed. Sew leather straps on the cover of the basket inside, for holding knife, fork and spoon.

Put a strap around the basket that you may hang from it a little pail containing cold soups recommended for drinks in summer.

Cold puddings should be wrapped in strong writing paper, then in wrapping paper and pinned close.

COLD DINNERS FOR SUMMER.

1. Bread and butter.
Salad of potatoes and cold baked fish.
Cold boiled beef.
Molasses Cookies.
Apple Soup.

2. Corn Bread.
Ham Sandwiches.
Baked sweet apples.
Custard pie.
Plum Soup

3. Bread and butter.
Cold veal.
Hard boiled eggs.
Pickled beets.
Cherry Pie.

4. Chopped beef sandwiches.
Salad of Lima Beans.
Ginger Snaps.
Cottage Cheese.
Irish Moss Lemonade.

5. Graham bread.
Cold roast mutton.
Cucumbers and salt.
Pumpkin pie.
Soda cream.

6. Bread and butter.
Dried Beef. Crackers.
Cheese. Sponge cake.
Cold coffee.

COLD DINNERS FOR WINTER.

7. Bread.
Cold boiled pork.
Cold baked beans with mustard and vinegar.
Doughnuts.
Apple pie.
Cold coffee.

8. Yeast biscuits and butter.
Cold chicken.
Pickles.
Cold rice pudding.
Apples.

9. Cold soda biscuits.
Veal and ham sandwiches.
Saratoga potatoes.
Mince pie.

10. Biscuits and butter with honey.
Cold corn beef and rye bread.
Dried apple tarts.
Cheese.

11. Bread and butter.
Smoked Herring.
Pickled beans.
Gingerbread.
Apples.

12. Corn bread and butter.
Cold roast beef and white bread.
Bread and apple pudding.
Bread cake.

INDEX.

THE AMERICAN PUBLIC HEALTH ASSOCIATION,

Organized in 1872 by a few eminent sanitarians, has grown in fourteen years to be the strongest and ablest association of its kind in America, if not in the world, and contains in its list of members, physicians, lawyers, clergymen, teachers, engineers, architects, and representatives of other trades and professions. Its influence has been felt in the legislative halls of the nation, as well as in every state and territory, for the amelioration of sickness and suffering, and the prolongation of human life.

The fourteen large and elegant volumes it has published are in themselves a monument to American hygiene, while their precepts and teachings have been felt through all ranks and grades of society, from the workshop to the mansion of the millionaire. No library is complete in its literature of sanitation without these works.

Each member of the Association receives a copy of the annual volume free of expense. This work alone is worth more to any individual than the cost of membership.

EXTRACT FROM CONSTITUTION, Art. III.

The members of this Association shall be known as Active and Associate. The Executive Committee shall determine for which class a candidate shall be proposed. The *Active* members shall constitute the permanent body of the Association, subject to the provisions of the Constitution as to continuance in membership. They shall be selected with special reference to their acknowledged interest in or devotion to sanitary studies and allied sciences, and to the practical application of the same. The *Associate* members shall be elected with special reference to their general interest only in sanitary science, and shall have all the privileges and publications of the Association, but shall not be entitled to vote. All members shall be elected as follows:

Each candidate for admission shall first be proposed to the Executive Committee in writing (which may be done at any time), with a statement of the business or profession, and special qualifications, of the persons so proposed. On recommendation of a majority of the committee, and on receiving a vote of two thirds of the members present at a regular meeting, the candidate shall be declared duly elected a member of the Association. The annual fee of membership in either class, shall be five dollars.

PUBLICATIONS OF THE AMERICAN PUBLIC HEALTH ASSOCIATION.

PUBLIC HEALTH: Reports and Papers of the American Public Health Association. Volumes 1 to 14 inclusive and one volume to be issued annually. These volumes contain the papers presented at the annual meetings of the Association, with the discussions upon each, and constitute large and very handsome works. Each member of the Association is entitled to the annual volume. A small edition is also placed in the hands of the treasurer for sale. At the present time there are but few complete sets on hand, and these are being rapidly taken by libraries.

DISINFECTION AND DISINFECTANTS: Their Application and Use in the Prevention and Treatment of Disease, and in Public and Private Sanitation, by the Committee on Disinfectants, appointed by the American Public Health Association.

The following is the list of authors of this work: George M. Sternberg, M. D., Surgeon U. S. Army, and Fellow by Courtesy in the Johns Hopkins University; Joseph H. Raymond, M. D., Professor of Physiology and Sanitary Science in Long Island College Hospital; Victor C. Vaughan, M. D., Ph. D., Professor of Physiological Chemistry in the University of Michigan, and Member of the Michigan State Board of

Health; Charles Smart, M. D., Surgeon U. S. Army, and member of the National Board of Health; George H. Rohé, M. D., Professor of Hygiene in the College of Physicians and Surgeons, Baltimore; Joseph Holt, M. D., President of the Louisiana State Board of Health; Samuel H. Durgin, M. D., health officer of Boston; and J. R. Duggan, M. D.

The original experimental investigations made by these specialists are of great importance and value, and render this work the most complete and practical volume upon disinfection and disinfectants yet published. A large amount of original work is devoted to the various micro-organisms, and in determining the value of many of the so-called disinfectants and germicides. The biological work was conducted mostly at the Johns Hopkins University under the Supervision of Dr. Sternberg, and at the University of Michigan under Dr. Vaughan. Various apparatus used for disinfecting purposes, as well as the admirable quarantine system at New Orleans, are fully described and illustrated. The chapter on Ptomaines, by Dr. Vaughan, is of great value.

The labors and investigations of these gentlemen extended over a period of three years, and involved no inconsiderable expense.

The work consists of two hundred and sixty-five pages, with sixty-eight illustrations, printed upon very heavy paper made especially for this volume, and is elegantly bound in handsome English cloth. The price has been placed at the low figure of two dollars per volume. Sent postpaid on receipt of price.

LOMB PRIZE ESSAYS.

These exceedingly valuable essays, written by authors of great ability, and selected as the best out of many received in competition, by committees of award who were selected by the American Public Health Association, the Conference of State Boards of Health, and the National Board of Health, and whose names alone guarantee the high character of the works, are being placed before the public at cost, through means that are being furnished the American Public Health Association.

No. 1. Healthy Homes and Foods for the Working-Classes. By Prof. VICTOR C. VAUGHAN, M. D., Ann Arbor, Mich.

JUDGES:—Dr. E. M. Moore, Pres. State Bd. of Health, Rochester, N. Y.; Dr. C. W. Chancellor, Sec'y State Bd. of Health, Baltimore, Md.; Medical Director Albert L. Gihon, U.S. Navy, Washington, D. C.; Dr. J. H. Raymond, Health Commissioner, Brooklyn, N. Y.; Major Charles Smart, Surgeon U. S. A., Washington, D. C.

SYNOPSIS OF CONTENTS.

Location; the cellar; the walls; the floors; arrangement of rooms; the windows; heating and ventilation; water-supply; the disposal of waste: the surroundings; the care of the home; buying or renting a house; tenement-houses; foods and food stuffs; the nutritive value of foods; the economic value of foods. *Animal foods;*—general properties; methods of cooking meat; milk; butter; cheese. *Vegetable foods;*—cereals and grains; flour and meal; bread; pease and beans; potatoes; other vegetables; starches; sugars; fruits; nuts; vegetable oils; condiments; tea; coffee; chocolate.

8vo paper, 62 pp. Price 10 cts.

Same in English-German (alternate pages in German) .15.

No. 2. The Sanitary Conditions and Necessities of School-Houses and Scoool-Life. By D. F. LINCOLN, M. D., Boston, Mass.

JUDGES:—Hon. Erastus Brooks, LL. D., State Bd. of Health, New York; Dr. H. P. Walcott, State Bd. of Health, Lunacy, and Charity, Cambridge, Mass.; Dr. Granville P. Conn, Pres. State Bd. of Health, Concord, N. H.; John Eaton, Commissioner of Education, Washington, D. C.; Col. George E. Waring, Jr., C. E., Newport, R. I.

Site: dampness, the cellar, contamination of soil and air,

drainage, foundation walls, neighborhood, etc. Plan and arrangement of the building; architecture, doors, windows, recitation and class-rooms, stairways, fire escapes, etc. Ventilation and heating; amount of fresh air and cubic space required, introduction of fresh air, carbonic acid gas exhaled, dimensions of ventilating apparatus, size of flues, circulation of air in room, ventilating by steam power, "indirect" heating, testing atmosphere of school-room, source of air supply, water closets, ventilating-stoves, open windows, ventilators, etc. Sewerage: bad air dangerous to health, waste-pipes, traps, ventilation of traps, closets, flush tanks, urinals, privies, disinfectants. Hygiene of the eye: nearsightedness, rules for using the eyes, location of windows, type used in school-books, curtains, and blinds. School desks and gymnastics: construction of seats, physical training. Affections of the nervous system: competition for prizes, lack of exercise, dress. Contagious diseases in schools. Sanitary supervision. This work contains fifteen illustrations.

8vo paper, 38 pages. Price, 5 cts.

No. 3. **Disinfection and Individual Prophylaxis against Infectious Diseases.** By George M. Sternberg, M.D., Major and Surgeon U. S. A.

Judges:—Dr. S. H. Durgin, Health Officer, Boston, Mass.; Dr. J. E. Reeves, Sec'y State Bd. of Health, Wheeling, W.Va.; Dr. Gustavas Devron, Pres. Aux. San. Assn., New Orleans, La.; Prof. Richard McSherry, M. D., Baltimore, Md.; Prof. James L. Cabell, LL. D., University of Virginia, Va.

Disinfection; groups of disinfectants.

Group I.—1. Fire; 2. Steam under pressure; 3. Boiling water; 4. Chloride of lime; 5. Liquor, soda chlorinatæ; 6. Mercuric chloride.

Group II.—7. Dry heat; 8 Sulphur dioxide; 9. Carbolic acid; 10. Sulphate of copper; 11. Chloride of zinc; general directions for disinfection; disinfection of excreta, etc.; disinfection of person; disinfection of clothing and bedding;

disinfection of the sick room; disinfection of privy vaults, cess pools, etc.; hospitals; disinfection of water and articles of food; disinfection of ships; merchandise. Individual prophylaxis against infectious diseases; cholera; yellow fever; small-pox; scarlet fever; diphtheria; tuberculosis; typhoid fever; concluding remarks, etc.

This essay is undoubtedly the best ever written in the English language upon the prevention of disease, and ought to be placed in the hands of every family.

8vo paper, 40 pp. Price, 5 cts.

Same in English German (alternate pages in German) .10.

No. 4. The Preventable Causes of Disease, Injury, and Death in American Manufactories and Workshops, and the Best Means and Appliances for Preventing and avoiding Them. By George H. Ireland, Springfield, Mass.

Judges:—Dr. E. M. Hunt, Sec'y State Bd. of Health, Trenton, N. J.; Dr. A. N. Bell, Editor *Sanitarian*, New York City; Major George M. Sternberg, Surgeon, U. S. A., Baltimore, Md.; Major John S. Billings, LL. D., U. S. A., Washington, D. C.; Mr. W. P. Dunwoody, Secretary National Board of Health, Washington, D. C.

Construction of workshops; elevators; fire-escapes; sanitary condition; plumbing; ventilation; sunlight; heating; lighting; precaution against fires; dust in factories; ice supply; handling heavy goods; machinery; saws and moulding machines; grindstones; railroading; emergencies; contagious diseases; cleanliness; facilities for workmen, etc.

8vo paper, 20 pages. Price, 5 cts.

The four essays, in one volume of nearly two hundred large octavo pages, *thoroughly indexed*, bound in cloth, 50 cts.

The same printed upon extra heavy paper made especially for this edition, and bound in expensive brown cloth with gold and black finish, making an elegant and handsome volume, $0.75.

www.ingramcontent.com/pod-product-compliance
Lightning Source LLC
Chambersburg PA
CBHW030836270326
41928CB00007B/1078

* 9 7 8 3 7 4 4 7 9 2 3 1 8 *